PERILOUS JOURNEY

THE MENNONITE BRETHREN
IN RUSSIA 1860-1910

D1496137

PERSPECTIVES on MENNONITE LIFE and THOUGHT

PERSPECTIVES on MENNONITE LIFE and THOUGHT

PERILOUS JOURNEY

THE MENNONITE BRETHREN IN RUSSIA 1860-1910

JOHN B. TOEWS

Kindred Press

Winnipeg, MB Canada and Hillsboro, KS USA.

PERILOUS JOURNEY
The Mennonite Brethren in Russia, 1860-1910

Copyright © 1988 by the Centers for Mennonite Brethren Studies, Fresno, CA; Winnipeg, MB; and Hillsboro, KS.

Published simultaneously by Kindred Press, Winnipeg, MB R2L 2E5 and Kindred Press, Hillsboro, KS 67063

Cover design by Sleeping Tiger Artworks, Winnipeg, Manitoba.

Printed in Canada by Fraser Valley Custom Printers Inc., Chilliwack, B.C.

International Standard Book Number: 0-919797-78-4

PREFACE

The history of any movement is always complex and never simple. At best its dynamic can be only partially understood. If information abounds we can describe its activities and actions, but even then it is difficult to comprehend its "inner" values and aspirations, to perceive its "heart throb." Past human experience is not easily encapsuled by formulas, typologies or theories which propose simplistic explanations to complex situations. Yet the temptation to bring order to a chaotic sequence of events or pronounce a profound verdict on the collective accomplishments of a group is overwhelming. Historical judgements are tricky. It is best to tread softly and err on the side of caution.

The Mennonite Brethren living in the Russia of the 1860s and 1870s can only be understood in the context of the political, social and religious world in which they lived and the circumstances associated with its ongoing transformation. The surviving records, though far from complete, certainly allow a reconstruction of the major events associated with Brethren beginnings. Official documents tell of group concerns and aspirations. They clearly delineate the contentious issues which separated the dissenters from the mother church. Unfortunately there are virtually no documents which tell the "inside" story, which inform the reader of the private spiritual pathways which the early Brethren followed. This makes it virtually impossible to trace the course of the group's inner journey or to explain adequately some of its less desirable activities. At times the reform ideals they wished to proclaim were marred by human failings. The Brethren story is one of becoming and so the laudatory and the contradictory, the bad and the good are generously mixed. I have tried to tell both sides of the early Brethren story.

This study does not try to be all-embracing or comprehensive. The forces and influences shaping the new movement are fleetingly mentioned. I have probably oversimplified the complex Mennonite world which both nurtured and opposed the new movement. Though I had access to many and varied sources I occasionally selected a specific diary or journal to illustrate the major issues of an era or substantial shifts in the priorities of the Brethren. Only the material used directly in the narrative has been cited.

This slim volume will hopefully contribute to a better understanding of the dynamics which shaped the early Brethren experience in Russia and intensify the awareness of this tradition among both old and new adherents as well as the simply curious.

John B. Toews

CONTENTS

CHAPTER 1
ONE MAN'S WORLD

It was New Year's day, 1838. David Epp noted in his diary[1] that Mennonites gathered for worship in the villages of Einlage, Neu-Osterwick and Schoenhorst. In Chortitza, the district center, elder Jacob Dyck read the marriage, birth and death statistics of the previous year and preached the New Year sermon. The mood of the gathering invited the congregation to recall and reflect. Now, after almost half a century on the new frontier, the offspring of the original migrants and their children felt quite at home. They no longer feared the ravages of drought, locusts or the hostility of the indigenous people on whose land they had settled. It was good to be a Chortitza farmer—the new markets, the increased cash flow, the expanded farming operations. Farms seemed to change hands more frequently. Carriages, though still a rarity, appeared on village streets. Epp sensed a striving and aggressiveness among his fellow colonists. At times he was not sure it was all to the good.

David Epp's forebears had always lived in small agricultural villages, at least as far as he knew. In both Prussia and Russia governments granted religious toleration only in exchange for Mennonite farming skills. For centuries the state churches in Europe had difficulty dealing with dissenters who insisted that peace was always preferable to war, that the church of Christ must be voluntary in its membership and that church and state be separate. At times the cost of upholding these cherished beliefs included suffering and migration. In the opinion of the Epp family, settlement in Russia had brought freedom. The tsarist *Privilegium* allowed the practice of all Mennonite beliefs. Though the vast steppes of the Ukraine meant isolation for the recent migrants, they also brought security and liberty.

1

The outside world no longer threatened. It was replaced by an all-Mennonite world—the Chortitza settlement. Land, custom and belief were indistinguishably blended in the life of David Epp. Neither he nor his fellow villagers knew where one ended or the other began. It was difficult to separate the affairs of the village from the affairs of the church. Every issue, civil or religious, involved everyone. It was simply the normal order of things. As a minister and community leader, Epp began to record the various events and happenings in his diary as early as 1837. Few episodes escaped his notice.

David Epp was only vaguely aware of the outside world. There was the tsar, guardian of the privileges granted to the Mennonites upon entering Russia. A less remote power was the *Fuersorge Komitee* [Guardian Committee][2] in Odessa whose jurisdiction specifically included all the foreign colonies. Closer to home were the numerous German Catholic and Lutheran colonists. Even these remained strangers to Epp, for according to general policy all foreign settlers were segregated according to religion. He of course knew of the other Mennonites who had settled in the Molotschna some three decades ago. Occasionally small groups of migrants from Prussia or Poland still passed through Chortitza en route to this settlement. Three years earlier a large group of settlers from Prussia, led by their elder Wilhelm Lange, had arrived in the Molotschna to found the Gnadenfeld colony.

In Epp's Chortitza the average villager was naturally preoccupied by the demands of farming and the common problems associated with life in the village. Fortunately a long-standing pattern of religious liturgy and festivals regularly reminded him of his Christian commitment. Mennonites after all were pilgrims and strangers in this world. New Year's had barely passed when the community gathered to celebrate Epiphany (*Heilige Drei Koenige*). Services commemorating Easter, Pente-cost, Thanksgiving and Christmas ensured a large influx of settlers from smaller surrounding communities to Chortitza and Neuendorf, villages with large churches. In such established centers Sunday services were held on a weekly basis. The colonists in more remote villages usually met once or twice a month in the local school. In the Chortitza settlement elder Jacob Dyck, assisted by a number of *Lehrer* (teacher-ministers) like David Epp, preached in the various villages on a rotating basis.

Since their beginnings in the sixteenth century Mennonites had affirmed only two ordinances: the Lord's Supper and

Baptism. Both were considered sacred and holy but conveyed no special grace to the participants. Communion was a solemn affair for the Chortitza Mennonites. There was a concern with the quality of the inner life which possibly reflected an older Prussian custom in which all potential communicants engaged in a serious self-scrutiny before participation. In Chortitza all congregational members heard a preparatory sermon *(Vorbereitungspredigt)* on the Sunday prior to the celebration. Customary practice dictated that only the elder administered the ordinance. In David Epp's Chortitza of 1838 Jacob Dyck served some 280 members of his Chortitza congregation on February 6.[3] The following Sunday he shared the rite with 251 parishioners in Neuendorf. In each case, a sermon of praise and thanks *(Dankpredigt)* was preached on the following Sunday. Generally the Lord's Supper was celebrated only once or twice a year.

Baptismal services were held annually, usually on the Day of Pentecost. Preparations began well in advance, at least according to David Epp's diary. In Chortitza and Neuendorf the Sunday morning readings of the articles of faith commenced on March 20, 1838. The process was momentarily diverted as special worship assemblies marked the passing of Palm Sunday, Good Friday as well as Easter Sunday and Easter Monday. Tuesday was still considered a holiday though no services were held. Two weeks after Easter, Jacob Dyck in Chortitza and David Epp in Neuendorf presented the articles a second time.[4] At the third reading the following week 27 young people presented themselves for baptism in Neuendorf, 50 in Chortitza.[5] The following Sunday when the articles were presented for the fourth time the number of candidates increased to 31 and 58 respectively.[6] A week later, after the articles were read for the fifth time, the *Bruderschaft* (brotherhood meeting) in both villages officially voted to accept the candidates for baptism.[7] Now the young people began their catechism classes. In Neuendorf the sessions were conducted by David Epp, in Chortitza by elder Dyck.[8] On May 15 all candidates sat on the front benches and listened as the articles of faith were read for the sixth time.[9] Did they believe? Were they committed? The assembled young people responded affirmatively to elder Dyck's questions. The following Sunday the elder baptized 56 people in Chortitza, then travelled to Neuendorf where he baptized another 31. Immediately after the baptism, minister Penner reminded the Chortitza congregation of the communion service scheduled for the coming Sunday and preached the customary preparatory sermon.[10] On June 5 the Chortitza communion celebration numbered 432 participants, including 56 new members. Since only the elder presided at the ceremony, Neuendorf conducted its communion service a week later.

Baptism was always a spiritual highpoint in the life of the local congregation. The lengthy period of preparation taught treasured religious values to the young. As they memorized the catechism, precepts heard since childhood were fixed in their minds. In later years the annual reading of the articles reminded them of the commitment which they had made. As a yearly event baptism affirmed the Mennonite interpretation and practice of faith. Baptism spoke of continuity. It was comforting to see the young following the old traditions. The words read and spoken in the lengthy liturgical process, the candidate's pledges; the sight and sound of water as it was poured over the heads of the recipients—the ancient faith still lived! How comforting for mind and spirit.

The yearly rites of Baptism and the Lord's Supper reminded Chortitza Mennonites that faith was still their reason for being. By and large they were willing to apply its principles in the world of every day with its village politics and quarrels or its basic concerns with planting, harvesting and livestock raising. The Mennonites of the 1830s and 1840s were a frank and direct people who knew what faith demanded of them and what they expected of each other. There was no need for an extensive written law since the demands of public and private morality were implicitly understood. Decades and even centuries had produced a Christian fabric in which custom and religion were deeply interwoven. There was also an awareness, generationally nurtured, that the Sermon on the Mount must be applied to daily life and that the life of Christ was a model worthy of imitation.

For diary writer Epp it was natural that religion intervened in everyday life; Epp the farmer was also Epp the *Lehrer* (Teacher). He held this position for life unless he became guilty of a severe moral lapse or proved incompetent. Epp was not only a preacher and worship leader but also the guardian of public morality. Together with his fellow *Lehrer* and elected deacons, he participated in a ministerial council known as the *Lehrdienst*. Such respected community leaders were popularly addressed as *Ohms* and even the room in which they met for consultation came to be called the *Ohmsstuebchen* (Ohms' room). The jurisdiction of the *Lehrdienst* encompassed matters like public drunkenness, false rumors and even assault cases, providing they were not too serious. Virtually all indiscretions involving civil and at times

4

criminal law brought the villagers before the *Lehrdienst.* Major infractions were presented to the *Bruderschaft*, an assembly of all adult males having membership in the local church. Its decisions, reached after open discussion and debate, were final. Expulsion from the congregation not only meant a loss of face, but of the legal privileges associated with the greater Mennonite community. Though sparingly used, excommunication was an effective weapon in regulating Mennonite life and morality.

The diary supplies an explicit insight into the operations of the *Lehrdienst* and also provides one of the few surviving portraits of Russian Mennonite life around 1840. What major problems confronted the Chortitza Mennonites? According to Epp there were two: drunkenness and deviant sexuality. All instances of drunkenness came before the *Lehrdienst,* and as far as Epp was concerned there were too many. On September 9, 1837, the council heard that Daniel Loewen was "insubordinate, abusive, given to cursing and drinking strong brandy, which caused such behavior."[11] After lengthy discussion he promised to abstain from strong drink. The new year had scarcely begun when a number of young men stood before the council charged with drunkenness and disorderly conduct at the August fair *(Jahrmarkt)* in Niko-pol.[12] The matter was deferred to a later *Bruderschaft* at which the ten rowdies were excommunicated.[13] Epp lamented: "When will this dissolute, wild life in the community end?"[14] It was not to be. A few days later more men appeared before the *Lehrdienst* on charges of intoxication and fighting[15] and were expelled from the congregation the following Sunday.[16] Later in the summer elder Dyck delegated Epp to visit the Osterwick mayor in an effort to curb his alcoholism.[17] Pub fights, wife beatings, unbecoming boisterousness and even accidental death[18]—Epp associated all such incidents with excessive drinking. Being a serious person Epp at times overlooked the obviously humorous. After Aaron Peters and Gerhard Siemens had freely imbibed at the Michailov fair they boarded a coach for Chortitza and annoyed the other passengers with their drunken antics. In the coach was an Odessa supervisory official, bound for an inspection tour of Chortitza.[19] The carousing colonists were of course reported to the volost head John Siemens and the local *Lehrdienst* took appropriate action!

Reflecting on the year just past, Epp jotted his last entry for 1838. "The immorality of adolescent youth steadily increases as does the consumption—[should I say] swizzling—of brandy and the dancing at weddings."[20] Two years later he again lamented:

5

"Immoral conduct intensifies: there is fornication and licentious behavior. Dancing at weddings and annual fairs is the order of the day."[21] The following year he once more complained of the prevailing "drunkenness, adultery and fornication."[22]

A second major problem for Epp involved the question of sexual morality in the Chortitza settlement. His approach to the subject was candid. The perimeters of sexuality were clear: marriage was a part of the divine order and sexual activity was confined to the married state. Intercourse before marriage or adultery during marriage were considered serious offenses by the family, the clergy and the community as a whole. When a transgression was discovered or confession made, the matter received a preliminary airing in the *Ohmsstuebchen,* then it was brought before the *Bruderschaft.* At this level the community reaffirmed its norms by recommending immediate expulsion from the church. Later, if repentance and contrition were in evidence, the supplicant was usually readmitted.

Epp was deeply shocked in 1837. The instances of promiscuity and adultery which occurred in Rosengart were "unheard of until now."[23] The following years seemed even worse. The *Lehrdienst* was confronted by a number of distasteful situations: squelching false rumors accusing the schoolteacher Klippenstein of having an affair;[24] the seduction of an older bachelor with the object of forcing him to marry;[25] the Mennonite Friesen, separated from his wife, was ordered not to spend so much time with the widow Dyck.[26] Johann Brand broke off his engagement to the widow Wiebe after two public announcements. The *Lehrdienst,* viewing this as breach of promise, fined him 30 rubles.[27] Excommunications for known cases of adultery[28] and premarital sex[29] steadily increased. Never before had the community dealt with so many cases of illegitimacy: a Mennonite youth impregnated a Russian lass;[30] a Mennonite girl bore a son to a Russian lad and had the baby baptized in the Orthodox Church;[31] a new-born child exposed by its young mother became the first Mennonite infant murdered since the migration to Russia.[32] There were even worse cases of deviation: a father impregnated his step-daughter;[33] the *Lehrdienst* heard a case of sexual assault;[34] several cases of sodomy proved even more unpleasant.[35] Community norms were gravely violated by such incidents.

David Epp's position as a *Lehrer* made him the guardian of public morality in the broadest sense of the word. Unofficially he was a judge hearing civil or even criminal cases. He and other members of the *Lehrdienst* played that role when dealing with the violence associated with alcoholism or questions of sexual impropriety. Beyond these areas they were expected to perform a broad range of duties relating to child welfare, juvenile delinquency, public mischief, contract disputes, property rights, theft, school questions or the enforcement of village by-laws.

During July, 1837, a certain Goerz from Rosenthal had beaten another colonist. The *Lehrdienst* met in the *Ohmsstuebchen* following the Sunday service on July 31. Goerz promised to live more peaceably.[36] Johann Siemens, who had violated village tree-planting ordinances, had to apologize to the district council and its head.[37] Only two weeks earlier the same body met to approve the construction of two new churches and fixed the necessary levies to cover construction costs.[38] Another agenda item involved the hiring of a doctor for the Chortitza region.[39] Dr. von Grosheim moved into his new office in Neuenburg on November 23.

Generally the cases brought before the *Lehrdienst* were as varied as life itself; there were the two lads charged with the theft of brandy[40] and the Rosenthal villager accused of stealing a cow and an animal hide.[41] During 1842 Epp and his associates mediated disputes between two partners in a rental agreement[42] and reconciled a brother and brother-in-law.[43] During the remainder of the year the *Lehrdienst* investigated the theft of a lamb and a quantity of rye flour from the local schoolteacher;[45] supervised an estate division;[46] and disciplined an employee who stole from his employer,[47] as well as a villager who refused to pay his church dues.[48] In another instance during April, 1843, Mrs. Abraham Reimer of Schoenhorst, whose nonresistance momentarily lapsed, beat not only the child of the village herdsman, but his wife as well. The law was no respecter of persons: she was fined ten rubles and excommunicated from the congregation.

Excommunications, however unpleasant, were an essential part of Kingdom activity for Epp. Individually and collectively the Mennonites were on a serious religious pilgrimage. Most understood the conditions of that journey. There was no need to spell out its inner dynamics or precisely outline the pattern of faith. Epp's sermons reminded his listeners of the essentials. He spoke of the "Son of Man who came to save,"[49] of the need for repentance,[50] the importance of faith[51] and the comfort of a Christ who sustains.[52] Epp implicitly believed in the necessity of a spiritual transformation, but nowhere in his diary does he indicate whether this involved an instantaneous, cataclysmic experience or if it involved a gradual affirmation of faith. All Epp's sermons assumed an inner experiential awareness of Christ which must be expressed in the practical everyday world.

Sunday worship was crucial in sustaining this view of the Kingdom. What inner spiritual journey did worship inspire in the Russian Mennonites of the mid-nineteenth century? Certainly they came to ascribe to God supreme worth, to stand in awe of His holiness, and to prostrate themselves in His presence. As the Old Testament was read they envisaged a God before whom the nations trembled. Their hymns too spoke of His glory, greatness, majesty and might. Yet the faith of their forefathers also included an all-gracious God revealed in the Son. Here was not only mercy but an invitation to imitate Christ's lifestyle. Perhaps this inclined Mennonite worship towards the functional and the pragmatic and focused it on the tangible and the concrete. The Christian community after all proclaimed the character of God by its daily walk. If godliness expressed itself in the context of community there was little need for the awe-inspiring or the mystical and the mysterious in worship.

For David Epp and his co-religionists the Gospel had to be actualized in daily life. The task was unending yet indispensible, for faith and practice were one. There was a temptation to be pragmatic: to participate faithfully in simple liturgy of Sunday services; to join in the occasional celebration of the Lord's Supper; to listen to the annual reading of the articles of faith and witness the annual baptismal rite. There was no need to pursue private religious ecstacy since special experiences were not the ultimate measure of spirituality. One only came to God with one's brother and sister. Through a common commitment to love, co-operation and orderly living the congregation tried to mirror a bit of God's Kingdom.

Every life situation, personal or collective, which limited the church's ability to reflect the fullness of the Kingdom had to be addressed—sometimes gently, sometimes vigorously. This did not mean that Epp's parishioners, by their spiritual perfection, desired to create a utopia or that they believed in salvation by works. The church was a human institution with human limitations. Some violated the norms of the Kingdom by lapses in faith and morality. Disputes and divisions were inevitable. The community, as an act of love directed its ailing member to the correct pathway. For Epp the *Lehrdienst* and *Bruderschaft* were useful agencies for this task.

Epp's assessment of Mennonite piety may have been too one-sided. Like any court of law the members of the *Lehrdienst* began to view the community in terms of the transgressors which appeared before it. Confronted only by sinners Epp perchance lost sight of the many saints committed to a life of discipleship. However grave their offences the accused represented a very small segment of the community.

Yet from Epp's personal standpoint the struggle for goodness seemed unending. There were moments of pain and despair as the list of offenders appearing before the *Lehrdienst* steadily increased. Was the intent of the Gospel, Epp wondered, really understood by the community? "How the light of the Gospel has been obscured in so many folk," he lamented in 1837. "When will the dawn of true enlightenment begin to break among us."[53] Early in 1838 he felt even more distressed. "Godlessness increases because love grows cold."[54] "When will the dissolute, wild life in the community end? When will the night of sin vanish?"[56] By 1841 he was even more pessimistic. "Immoral conduct steadily intensifies. Fornication, licentious behavior and dancing at weddings and annual fairs is the order of the day... There is no thought of repentence and conversion."[57] Epp's pessimism continues in one of the last entries of the surviving diary. "Spiritually the community is in a drowsy state: drunkenness, adultery and fornication are prevalent as are lies and gossip."[58]

Unknown to Epp, spiritual revival had already begun on the Russian steppes.

NOTES

[1] David Epp Diary (Mennonite Heritage Centre, Winnipeg, Manitoba.

[2] The colonists usually used this shortened form. Its full title was "Das Fuersorge Komitee der auslaendischen Kolonisten Sued-Russlands."

[3] David Epp Diary, February 6, 1838.

[4] April 10, 1838.

[5] April 17, 1838.

[6] April 24, 1838.

[7] May 1, 1838.

[8] May 8, 1838; May 12, 1838.

[9] In the later decades of the nineteenth century it was customary to hear the entire confession of faith two or three times before the baptismal ceremony. Approximately half the document was read each Sunday. Epp's report of six readings probably reflects that practice.

[10] May 22, 1838.

[11] September 9, 1837.

[12] January 27, 1838.
[13] February 27, 1838.
[14] *Ibid.*
[15] March 3, 1838.
[16] March 6, 1838.
[17] August 21, 1838.
[18] February 22, 1842.
[19] July 2, 1842.
[20] December 26, 1838.
[21] December 31, 1841.
[22] December 27, 1842.
[23] December 26, 1837.
[24] July 14, 1838.
[25] March 26, 1838.
[26] November 6, 1841.
[27] November 20, 1841.
[28] March 6, 1838; April 28, 1842; September 23, 1842; March 21, 1843.
[29] October 22, 1838; October 30, 1838; December 7, 1841; January 10, 1843.
[30] February 22, 1842.
[31] November 15, 1841.
[32] July 2, 1841. On illegitimacy see also April 23, 1839; August 17, 1841.
[33] March 5, 1839.
[34] August 7, 1841.
[35] April 20, 1838; September 14, 1841.
[36] July 31,1837.
[37] *Ibid..*
[38] July 18, 1837.
[39] *Ibid.*
[40] March 12, 1839.
[41] April 5, 1839.
[42] February 19, 1842.
[43] April 15, 1842.
[44] May 3-5, 1842.
[45] July 2, 1842.
[46] July 16, 1842.
[47] September 23, 1842.
[48] September 24, 1842.
[49] August 8, 1837.
[50] July 31, 1837; August 28, 1837.
[51] November 7, 1837; September 7, 1841.
[52] September 5, 1837; September 26, 1837.
[53] July 15, 1837.
[54] January 27, 1838.
[55] February 27, 1838.
[56] March 6, 1838.
[57] December 31, 1841.
[58] December 27, 1842.

CHAPTER II
EXPANDING HORIZONS

There was a sense of isolation and loneliness associated with David Epp's struggle for faith and discipleship. Villages, not to mention settlements, rarely knew what was happening beyond their borders. Judging from his jottings, Epp was unaware of earlier expressions of Mennonite piety or even of contemporary spiritual aspirations in the nearby Molotschna settlement.[1] There was a sense in which Chortitza, as the oldest Mennonite colony in Russia, clung to a narrower religious-cultural tradition. There appeared to be contentment with what had been and what was. Perhaps it was not so much resistance to change as a conservative view of what it really meant, in the words of St. Augustine, to build the City of God.

David Epp was apparently not aware that a group of his co-religionists were taking the City of God very seriously. The *Kleine Gemeinde* had emerged in the Molotschna settlement in 1812 amid less than auspicious circumstances.[2] Though the Molotschna colonists had settled on better land, with more capital and under rather promising conditions, they seemed less content. Resolves for a peaceful co-existence were put to the test when one early elder, Jacob Enns, began correcting the erring members of his flock. Instead of admonishing them in love he resorted to corporal punishment and even imprisonment. Apparently the preaching of the Word no longer deterred dishonesty, debauchery and violence. Concerned parishioners argued that the Scriptures called for spiritual not physical discipline. Unfortunately Jacob Enns proved an insensitive elder given to vindictive action against those who opposed him. As the dissident leader Klaas Reimer expressed it: "...so many evil works emanated from the elder that it was necessary for us to leave their fellowship."[3]

11

The ecclesiastical establishment led by Enns not only excommunicated the rebels but in cooperation with civilian powers even threatened exile to Siberia. The small group, which had earlier met for Bible study and prayer, was forced to hold its own worship services. Sporadic encouragement came from other more moderately inclined Molotschna leaders and eventually the dissidents obtained a measure of legal recognition.

The surviving documents make one thing clear. The secessionists were primarily concerned that the established church used civil means for disciplining church members. For Klaas Reimer and his associates this violated nonresistance since it involved the use of violence. They had another concern. The true church of Christ must find expression in a restricted setting. Mennonite backsliding was associated with the accumulation of wealth and economic power, the participation in the magistry and the lapse of the nonresistance principle. Restitution was only possible through separation in order "that our church could be led back to the foundation and original constitution of the church."[4] "Kleine Gemeinde" not only implied a small part of the whole but a committed church, a faithful remnant.

What, in the opinion of the secessionists, was essential to the restitution of faith? They stressed the necessity of repentance and spiritual rebirth though they did not hold particularly dramatic views on the exact nature of the salvation experience. Discipleship expressed itself in the context of the local congregation and took issue with the besetting sins of the community such as dishonesty, violence and material extravagance. The church must strive for purity. In this context the exercise of spiritual discipline was essential.

These serious believers also held that the pure church must be nurtured by pure doctrine. They were concerned with the corrupting religious ideas permeating the Mennonite world via "alien books published by other confessions."[5] Some elders in Prussia and Russia were apparently avid readers of pietistic literature emanating from Germany. Klaas Reimer was especially apprehensive about the popularity of Johann Bengel (1687-1752). While Mennonite readers may have sanctioned his views on biblical authority, spiritual rebirth and the life of sanctification, they should, Reimer felt, be wary of his undue eschatological speculation. Bengel saw the book of Revelation as a precise outline of future events and boldly produced a chronology which set Christ's coming for 1836. Some Mennonite ministers and elders, Reimer felt, were surely courting danger in their preoccupation with Christ's thousand year reign on earth. The Kingdom had higher priorities than theological speculation.

The pure church after all drank from pure waters, especially the writings of its Anabaptist-Mennonite forebears. Spiritual perimeters were best sustained by reading Menno Simons' *Foundation of Christian Doctrine*, the confessions of faith or the *Martyrs' Mirror*. Other writings like Peter Peters' *Mirror of Greed* or Dirk Philips' *Handbook* were likewise a secure guide to faith, especially on the practice of nonviolence. The *Kleine Gemeinde* effort to provide wholesome nurture for the Mennonite soul was not too successful. Some ministers and elders simply refused to read more broadly, others remained intrigued with the more liberal teachings of pietism and began to wonder if infant baptism, the participation in the military and the swearing of oaths really constituted apostasy.[6] The offer of purer nourishment was not widely accepted and the flirtation with pietism continued. In the decades to come the love affair would be both corrupting and redeeming.

Kleine Gemeinde dissent left a mixed legacy. The dislocation associated with migration, the new frontier and the lack of spiritual leadership had resulted in a societal destabilization which the protesters described as "debauchery, fighting, lying and cheating."[7] Since collective reform was out of the question those with righteous aspirations left the *Grosze Gemeinde*. Once outside they were obligated to define both the terms of individual discipleship and the standards of the pure church. The aspirations of moderates and conservatives among the dissidents did not always harmonize. It was also difficult to forge a new peoplehood amidst the existing though admittedly deficient people of God in the larger community. *Kleine Gemeinde* leaders derived their model for the restitution of the church from Scripture and the Christian values and ethics contained in Anabaptist literature. In their insistence upon a separated, pure church the protesters ministered in a prophetic role to the larger Mennonite community. It was a loving confrontation which insisted that the Kingdom fared miserably when it condoned worldly values or when it allowed lax standards among its members. The sincere Mennonite pilgrim never separated faith and life.

In his diary David Epp does not mention the Mennonite teacher Tobias Voth (1791-?). He had lived at another time and in another place. Voth left his native Brandenburg around 1820 to teach school in Ohrloff, a Molotschna village some one hundred miles southeast of Chortitza. Epp knew of the school, but not of its first teacher. Several years before leaving for Russia, Tobias and his wife, influenced by the writings of the pietist Jung-Stilling, underwent a new life experience. He subsequently strove for a piety which in his own words was preoccupied with "the state of the heart and what man may have in Jesus as Savior."[8] Most of his contemporaries were apparently content with less. Voth's tenure at the Ohrloff school, which was to infuse Christian ideals into the Mennonite community, ended in 1829. His autobiography reflects a lonely man, disillusioned by the people he came to serve. Contemplative and inward-looking, he seemed irrelevant in a Mennonite world concerned with frontier survival. Neither his reading society (*Leseverein*) nor his prayer meetings for missions endured for long.[9]

David Epp also makes no reference to the recently deceased missions promoter and small group fellowship advocate, elder Franz Goerz of Rudnerweide. Occasional visits to the Molotschna apparently did not bring Epp into contact with British and Foreign Bible Society supporters like elder Peter Wedel of Alexanderwohl and Bernhard Fast of Ohrloff. He also does not speak of the refreshing piety of the Prussian migrants who settled in Gnadenfeld in 1835. There is another sense of isolation. The diary contains only two references to books. Epp mentions the arrival of 900 hymnals from Prussia and notes his relationship with the British Bible Society representative John Melville.[10] Thanks to Melville's influence David became the Chortitza Bible distributor for the Society.[11]

Epp's diary probably leaves the reader with a distorted sense of the loneliness of the Russian steppe. It was, to be sure, still a new frontier in which the struggle for survival was a high priority. Yet, almost imperceptibly, the Mennonite world was changing. The Quakers, William Allen and Stephen Grellet, visited the colonies some two decades before John Melville. Other visitors to Chortitza included the emigrants from Prussia whose ongoing presence brought news of a steadily changing Mennonite world to the west. And what of the impact of pietistic and other religious literature also coming from the west and its dissemination via the lively familial, ministerial and economic contacts between the two colonies? In the end this material and the spirituality it promoted proved irrepressible.

There were other changes. While in the Molotschna colony during 1838, David Epp visited the school in Ohrloff taught by Heinrich Heese, as well as a newly built school in Steinbach directed by Friedrich Lange.[12] He was so impressed that he resolved to send his son to Steinbach the following year.[13] Not long after, Epp was astounded to hear that Heese received an annual salary of 800 rubles, a free house plus other benefits.[14] There was also a rumor that Heese himself was extremely unhappy about the local school situation.[15] Though there was still a general lack of support and commitment the interest in schools was there to stay. Chortitza elected a School Commission and instructed it to draw up appropriate statutes.[16] It seemed the long dark night was finally over.

Judging from the diary, David Epp's religious world was still a secure and cohesive one. He records no debates about theology or dissent in the pattern of religious expression. Chortitza seemed content with its annual festivals and liturgies. Faith was fixed and known. Epp did not sense the same contentment among his co-religionists in the Molotschna settlement. During his annual visits to the colony he was repeatedly informed of the prevailing civil and religious disputes.[17] Why were these settlers so volatile and discontented? Compared with the Chortitza colonists their conditions of settlement were more tolerable. They had only begun to arrive in 1804. By then bureaucratic procedures related to colonization had been streamlined. Then, too, the flow of immigrants from Prussia was a gradual one, lasting several decades. Many arrived with substantial inventory and larger cash reserves than had been the case in Chortitza. Perhaps economic inequality accounted for some of the unhappiness. The impoverished seeking new opportunities could not compete with the wealthy who coveted even greater riches on the new frontier. There was another element. The gradual influx brought Mennonites from many different localities in Prussia. Ecclesiastical practices occasionally differed from region to region and at times there were even minor theological variations. Several decades often separated migrants from the same area. If local religious and intellectual views changed in the interval, the new settler might even offend his co-religionist who had preceded him by twenty or thirty years.

In most instances the status quo was preferable to change. In David Epp's Chortitza of 1839 elder Jacob Dyck declared that "the girls were not to wear their braids to the side nor should young men have long hair over their forehead or their hair completely shorn in the neck"—all this was vanity. In the same year there was further consternation when several local teachers

15

erected Christmas trees in the schools and asserted that gift-giving was appropriate. Some likened this to image worship.[18] It was even difficult to be innovative in the Molotschna. The Ohrloff elder Berhard Fast, a prime supporter of the Ohrloff school and a strong advocate of Russian Bible Society endeavors, was confronted by angry parishioners when he admitted a visiting missionary to the communion service. Three-quarters of his congregation left him in the 1820s. All was not lost. His orphaned congregation in Ohrloff, aided by progressive elements in Rudnerweide and Alexanderwohl, became something of an oasis for ongoing religious vitality.

It was now time for the Lutherans to help the Mennonites in Russia. In faraway Brandenburg, a gifted family named Lange had left the Lutheran church and joined the Mennonite congregation in Brenkenhofswalde. Their son Wilhelm had already been ordained a Mennonite elder in 1810. A man of broad-ranging religious interests, Lange was in contact with the Moravians in Prussia, especially one Gottlieb Jahr. Almost a century later, when the Russian Mennonite historian Peter M. Friesen read two Brenkenhofswalde confessions of faith copied by Wilhelm in 1812 and 1815, he was "amazed at the theological training and broad classic religious insights which these simple farmer-bishops... developed."[19] Forty families led by Lange left Brenkenhofswalde for the Molotschna in 1835. They settled in Gnadenfeld, a village soon known for its mission and Bible study groups. Not all Mennonites were impressed by their religious zeal. Some referred to the new settlers as "fanatics" and "goody-goodys."[20]

For the next decade and a half Gnadenfeld dominated religious-cultural developments in the Molotschna. It was an improbable sequence. Moravians with their emphasis on evangelism and the enjoyment of personal salvation significantly influenced Mennonites and Lutherans in Prussia. Lutherans with names like Strauss, Klatt, Rabe and Lenzmann affiliated with the Mennonites and joined them in an eastward migration.[21] The imported piety generated a type of redemption for other Mennonites in the Molotschna. This was especially the case when Friedrich W. Lange, a younger relative of Wilhelm, succeeded him in 1841. The new school in Steinbach to which David Epp sent his son reflected a segment of this dynamic religious-cultural energy. Unfortunately scandalous rumors involving Friedrich led to his resignation in 1849. The congregation remained without a leader until 1854. What happened to its cohesiveness and sense of common purpose in the interval? Did this affect its stability in the early 1860s? No lesser figure than Bernhard Fast, who may have resented the popularity of these "foreigners" or simply acted with characteristic impetuosity, figured in Lange's deposition.[22] The sins which Bernhard Fast and his fellow Mennonites committed against the former Lutherans were not laid to their charge. Though the Molotschna settlement experienced a spiritual and cultural leveling off during the next decade, the "Gnadenfeld enlightenment" endured in both the spiritual seekers and teachers it produced.

Schools, books, dynamic religious leaders and new migrants were not the only realities in the Chortitza and Molotschna settlements. While David Epp was intensely preoccupied with building the City of God many of his fellow Mennonites focused on erecting the earthly city. Possession and accumulation here and now seemed more assuring than the vagaries of the world to come. A new hero appeared on the Russian steppes—the man with land and money. Usually he found it easy to transform economic to political power. His performance with its entrepreneurship, productivity and accumulation was a convincing model for a new kind of kingdom building.

It became more difficult to distinguish between the two kingdoms. The earthly city demanded a greater say in the building of the heavenly one. Often it hid under the guise of nominal piety by strongly endorsing long-standing patterns associated with worship and congregational life. Though such orthodoxy appeared to uphold traditional religion it was just as easily a demand for conformity in the interests of the Mennonite state. Religious stability and constancy, it was assumed, ensured progress and development.

All too frequently the assumption that the City of God would endorse mundane priorities proved correct. In South Russia the European demand for grain generated increased capital inflow. Those with land naturally benefited. Unfortunately, rapid population growth a few decades after settlement not only absorbed reserve lands but ensured a landless class which soon comprised approximately two-thirds of the population. In the Molotschna, population growth in the later 1850s clearly illustrates the problem. As of January 1st, 1856,[23] the settlement (48 villages) numbered 17,516; by 1860 it stood at 20,828; in 1865 it reached 24,235.[24] While the total population still stood at 17,516 the colony listed 2,059 landless families compared to 1,188 with land. Assuming an average family size of five there was only

17

enough land to support a population of 5,940 in a system where indivisible farmsteads were the rule.[25] What kind of pressures existed when the population stood at 20,828 or 24,235? Systematic colonization under the supervision of the mother colony only began in the late 1860s, and even then only under pressure from the Russian government.

Since the right to vote was tied to land holding, the emergence of a centralized, more authoritarian leadership was inevitable. The landowning class invariably placed its own members into key positions. Mennonite elders, at times elected on the assumption that their farms made them economically self-sufficient, participated in the growing prosperity of the mid-nineteenth century. Increasingly their interests coincided with the rich and powerful. It had always been assumed that the elder reflected the priorities of the community that elected him. Now, as wealth brought independence, that no longer seemed to be the case. The earliest attempts to centralize ecclesiastical power took place during the 1820s in the Molotschna when the elders of the Ohrloff, Alexanderwohl and Rudnerweide congregations united. They were joined somewhat later by the elders of the Waldheim and Gnadenfeld congregations. The consolidation process culminated in 1851 with the formal organization of the *Kirchen-konvent* (Ecclesiastical Council). From the very onset its instincts were administrative and legal, rather than visionary and creative. The council rather that the community became the supreme arbitrator of most religious problems. In such a setting, pleas for deeper piety or free religious inquiry were often interpreted as a threat to the elders' leadership.[26]

Since the leaders of church and state increasingly reflected the same economic interests it was easy for them to cooperate in other areas. Though power in the Mennonite world was vested in two authorities, it readily shifted in either direction. It was soon evident that within this diarchy the elders held the lesser sway. On May 26, 1842, David Epp confided the following to his diary.

> Elder Jacob Dyck has received a communication from elder Bernhardt Fast in Halbstadt. It included a letter addressed to Fast by Johann Cornies, Ohrloff. In it elder Jacob Dyck is ordered not to involve himself in any ecclesiastical matters by his excellency state counsellor Eduard von Hahn of the Supervisory Commission in Odessa. If there is unrest in Warkentin's church the agitators are to be reported to the state counsellor.

Warkentin is to be taken into custody and [transported] to Orechov [for his part in the unrest.]27

Epp made two other references to von Hahn in 1842. The state counsellor demanded to know the exact title of the hymnal elder Jacob Dyck was importing from Prussia as well as the individual titles of the songs.28 The second entry was more foreboding.

The elder Jacob Warkentin of Altonau has been deposed from his office by state counsellor von Hahn on account of the disobedience of the church and other disputes. Four elders were elected upon orders of the state counsellor.29

Warkentin's ecclesiastical jurisdiction included almost three-quarters of the Molotschna population. He apparently resisted "progressive" measures issued by the estate owner Johann Cornies, head of the Agricultural Union. Eduard von Hahn proved a willing ally. Acting only on the authority of the Odessa Supervisory Commission he illegally deposed Warkentin. Warkentin's religious jurisdiction was then divided among the newly elected elders. Apparently there was no protest from other Mennonite leaders.

Unchallenged, the earthly city continued its aggressive tactics. Elder Heinrich Wiens of Margenau had excommunicated several of his members who assisted in the corporal punishment of a youth on orders of the local mayor. Angered by this intrusion into civil jurisdiction Hahn ordered Wiens to appear before him in Halbstadt on July 20, 1846. Since the Mennonite *Privilegium* guaranteed religious freedom Wiens argued, he had the right to discipline his own members. Hahn held that ministers, like others in the community, must submit to civic authority.30 When elder Wiens protested, Hahn reminded him that he was "only a farmer with 65 dessiatines of land and as a farmer was subject to the mayor and also not exempt from corporal punishment."31 He threatened to make official representations aimed at abolishing the *Privilegium* if the other elders continued to support Wiens. If their intentions were honorable, they must depose Wiens. The elders capitulated. By threatening loss of privileges, imprisonment and even physical punishment the earthly city won the day. In a sense Johann Cornies typified the priorities of the earthly city. He advocated an efficient economy capable of responding to expanding international markets and an education

19

system capable of preparing the young Mennonite for the broader world. Though he never denied the existence of the heavenly city, his activities eventually relegated its champions, the congregational leaders, to a lesser role.

The elders had played into the hands of the Mennonite state and so established something of a precedent for dealing with religious nonconformity. If there was still a line of demarcation between religion and politics the initiative now lay with civic officials. By and large the elders submitted without protest. When the Molotschna Brethren seceded from the old church in 1860 district chairman David Friesen felt entirely within his rights when he ordered close surveillance of the dissenters. In a report to Friesen in 1860 the Molotschna elders listed the concerns of the protesters: the apostacy of the existing church; the need for a separate observance of the Lord's Supper; the importance of personally understanding the Scriptures. The elders nevertheless argued for the suppression of the group. "We cannot give our consent to the formation and existence of a free and new religious fellowship within our Mennonite community." 32 Further action was left to the discretion of civil officials, for the elders did not wish to specify what other "treatment or punishment be applied."33 Like exasperated medieval bishops they turned the unrepentant heretics over to the state. Dialogue and conciliation seemed out of the question. The state easily confronted deliberate, public nonconformity. It was, however, powerless to control another kind of inner journey which drew its nourishment from the printed word.

Economic progress, though narrowing the base of political power, contributed to a modest revival of schools and learning. In 1838 David Epp was enthusiastic about his visit to Heinrich Heese's Ohrloff school and Friedrich Lange's newly erected school in Steinbach. The next decade did not bring universal public education to the Mennonite colonies but it was a beginning. If the aspirations of the teacher and the community were compatible, an elementary school might flourish for decades. At first most schools were only an extension of village priorities and left much to be desired in terms of curriculum and facilities. Grim portraits of indifferent teachers, limited course content, and stultifying methodology have survived from the first half of the nineteenth century.34 Many students nevertheless learned to read and write. In the end that was all that mattered. Serious seekers could now read serious books and some did. Ironically, the diffusion of reading and writing skills funded by the earthly city soon resulted in a defiance of its dominance. The enlightened leaders of the *Kleine Gemeinde* had been ahead of their time.

In part this challenge emerged from the elementary school curriculum which always included *Biblische Geschichte* (Bible stories). This practice of "knowing the stories" laid the foundation of a sound biblical literacy in later life. The long term impact of such classroom accumulation was significant. Among the early Brethren, knowledge of the Bible was amazingly sophisticated. In their reminiscences these men and women usually credited caring and deeply religious village school teachers for this legacy.

During the first half of the nineteenth century Mennonite readers in Russia were few and far between and the materials they read relatively restricted. What books other than the Bible did the first migrants bring with them? A Tobias Voth may have immersed himself in the works of Jung-Stilling but that did not mean that such sophistication was widespread. By the mid-century Mennonite spirituality was not only nurtured through the Netherlandic legacy advocated by *Kleine Gemeinde* leaders, but solace for the Mennonite soul was also found in Johann Schabalies, *The Journeying Soul*, a German equivalent of *Pilgrim's Progress*, and the pietistical work, *True Christianity*, by Johann Arndt. The era constituted something of a watershed with regard to the availability of religious materials. In 1840 elder Benjamin Ratzlaff in Rudnerweide wrote to the Chortitza elder Jacob Hildebrandt about a proposed hymnal not yet in print.[35] No other books were mentioned. Twenty years later Jacob Martens of Tiegenhagen addressed two concerns to the same elder: he was sending copies of *Das Mennonitische Blatt* published in Philadelphia, the *Sueddeutsche Warte*, and some news appearing in *Der Volksfreund* printed in Koenigsberg; secondly he was enclosing some religious pamphlets left by the English Bible agent John Melville.[36]

The Molotschna teacher and minister Dietrich Gaeddert provides another insight into the expanding cultural-religious awareness. When the guest speaker failed to arrive for an 1860 Sunday service in Rueckenau, Gaeddert felt it appropriate to read a sermon from the Wuerttemberg pietist Ludwig Hofacker (1797-1828).[37] Some years later after he had been ordained Gaeddert began to read the sermons of the Mennonite minister Jacob Denner (1659-1746). On at least one occasion he read from Spurgeon's sermons. There are only two references to books in the entire diary: in 1860 he bought a copy of the new choral book while in 1862 he records that the local school "society has obtained twelve books for us school teachers to examine."[38] There was one reference to periodic literature. Gaeddert subscribed to the *Volksbote* and *Sonntagsblatt* early in 1871.[39]

The expansion of Gaeddert's intellectual and religious horizon was enhanced by two other influences. First, he regularly attended the mission conferences held annually at Gnadenfeld. The second involved the 1868 preacher at that festival, Heinrich Dirks, the first missionary sent out by the Russian Mennonites under the Dutch Mennonite Board of Missions. Dirks studied at the Missionshaus Barmen, Germany, between 1862-66. On August 19, 1869, over 3,000 people attended the Gnadenfeld church for Dirks's ordination as elder and missionary.[40] The presence of Dirks introduced Gaeddert to a new preaching style which he greatly admired and possibly to a new theology related to missions and eschatology.[41] When the two had shared the pulpit two weeks earlier, Gaeddert was amazed how Dirks sketched "the course of the Kingdom of God since Adam" and pointed to the culmination of God's plan—the millenium, the anti-Christ, Gog and Magog, the destruction of the earth.[42] Dirks preached on "the marriage of the Lamb" and the "new Jerusalem" on August 24. On the same evening Gaeddert went to visit elder Buller and was surprised to find Dirks present. It was a pleasant visit during which Dirks "drew me a chart of the plan of God's kingdom."[43]

Mennonite Brethren beginnings cannot be separated from a broad-based cultural ferment involving schools, books, periodic mission festivals and visiting speakers. It constituted a formative force in the emergence of the movement and permeated all of Mennonite society in the decades which followed. Dietrich Gaeddert's theological growth not only included his exposure to Dirks' emphasis on missions and eschatology but the frequent readings of Hofacker's and Denner's salvation-oriented sermons. Men like Dirks and Gaeddert remained in the old church. For them new wine could be poured into old wineskins. The increased circulation of the printed word became a formidable threat to a community inclined to celebrate the values of earthly paradise. Most of the available material was religious in character. By focusing passionately on the City of God the reading pilgrim deliberately or inadvertently challenged the prevailing structure and values.

NOTES

1. David Epp Diary (Mennonite Heritage Centre, Winnipeg, Manitoba), February 2, 1839.

2. Many of the documents relating to the emergence of the *Kleine Gemeinde* have recently been published for the first time in Delbert Plett, *The Golden Years: The Mennonite Kleine Gemeinde in Russia 1812-1849*, (Steinbach, Manitoba, 1985).

3. *Ibid.*

4. *Ibid.*, 223.

5. *Ibid.*, 225.

6. *Ibid.*, 280.

7. *Ibid.*, 196.

8. P.M. Friesen, *Die Alt-Evangelische Mennonitische Bruderschaft in Russland*, 1789-1910 (Halbstadt, 1911).

9. Documents published in Friesen contain an autobiography, memorandum and excerpts from several letters. *Ibid.*, 569-77.

10. See James Urry, "John Melville and the Mennonites: A British Evangelist in South Russia, 1837-c.1875," *Mennonite Quarterly Review*, LIV (1980), no. 4, 305-322.

11. David Epp Diary, July 19, 1842. Epp recorded that he accepted six "chests" of Bibles and New Testaments for distribution in the Chortitza settlement.

12. *Ibid.*, September 20, 1838.

13. *Ibid.*, January 17, 1839. Epp made a second visit to both schools early in 1839. See February 2, 1839.

14. *Ibid.*, May 27, 1841.

15. *Ibid.*, June 22, 1841.

16. *Ibid.*, July 7, 1841.

17. *Ibid.*, February 2, 1839.

18. *Ibid.*, April 30, 1839.

19. Friesen, 82.

20. *Ibid.*

21. "Aus der Gnadenfelder Gemeindechronik," *Mennonitisches Jahrbuch*, (1909), 109-10.

22. Friesen, 84.

23. J. Martens, "Statistische Mittheilungen ueber die Mennoniten-Gemeinden im suedlichen Russland," *Mennonitische Blaetter*, Vol. 4(1857), 33.

24. Figures recorded in the Dietrich Gaeddert Diary (Mennonite Library and Archives, N. Newton, Kansas). Read by the elder at the New Year service on January 1, 1861 and January 1, 1865.

25. Adolf Ehrt cites 5.18 as the average family size in *Das Mennonitentum in Russland* (Berlin, 1932), 54.

26. In David Epp's Chortitza the unofficial *Kirchenkonvent* still worked closely with local congregations. See for example January 27, 1838; January 30, 1841; July 9, 1841; October 30, 1841; November 27, 1841; January 14, 1842; April 15, 1842; July 2, 1842.

27. *Ibid.*, May 26, 1842.

28. *Ibid.*, July 2, 1842.

29. *Ibid.*, December 27, 1842.

30. Franz Isaak, *Die Molotschnaer Mennoniten* (Halbstadt, 1908), 117-121.

31 *Ibid.*, 119. On August 14, 1846 Hahn wrote to Mennonite civic leaders in the Molotschna stipulating that religious leaders must not involve themselves in secular affairs and that the primary duty of every citizen was "to obey the authorities appointed by the government." Ibid., 114-116.

32 Jacob P. Bekker, *Origin of the Mennonite Brethren Church* (Hillsboro, Kansas, 1973), 56.

33 *Ibid.*, 57.

34 John B. Toews, "The Mennonite Village School in Nineteenth Century Russia," *Journal of the American Historical Society of Germans from Russia,* Vol. 7(1984), no. 1, 27.36.

35 Mennonite Library and Archives (North Newton, Kansas). Benjamin Ratzloff to Elder Jacob Hildebrand, Rudnerweide, May 21, 1840.

36 Mennonite Library and Archives (North Newton, Kansas). Jacob Martens to Elder Jacob Hildebrand. Tiegenhagen, August 29, 1860.

37 Gaeddert Diary, August 21, 1860.

38 *Ibid.*, May 15, 1862.

39 *Ibid.*, January 5, 1871.

40 *Ibid.*, August 31, 1869.

41 *Ibid.*, August 19, 1869.

42 *Ibid.*, August 6, 1869.

43 *Ibid.*, August 24, 1869.

CHAPTER III
NEW BEGINNINGS

David Epp's diary faithfully reflected both his broader spiritual concerns and his personal pilgrimage. He understood the difficulties of bringing the entire Mennonite community into the church, yet believed that godliness must express itself in this context. He and his fellow ministers on the *Lehrdienst* (ministerial council) generally subscribed to a narrow pathway. His sermons imply that Epp believed in the importance of spiritual transformation but he was never explicit about the exact nature of that experience. Was one simply born into the Christian community and reared in the faith or was a dramatic rebirth essential? He never spoke specifically about *Bekehrung* (conversion) as a dramatic turnabout, yet constantly longed for *Busse* (repentance) and *Bekehrung* in his parish.[1]

Preoccupied with the daily problems of the visible Kingdom, Epp struggled to affirm the sufficiency of Christ but sometimes with a sense of desperation and at times pessimism. There was a working out of salvation with "fear and trembling," a reluctance to speak freely of liberating faith or of joy in the Lord. The diary suggests that mid-century Mennonite piety, while proclaiming the essentials of Christian salvation, lacked a firm conviction on the subject. It seemed one could never quite be sure.

In June, 1868, David's son Jacob, now also a minister, confided the following to his diary.

> Oh how perverse is my heart! How it vacillates between good and evil! How lukewarm is the love for the Lord Jesus! Oh Lord Jesus through Thy mighty power create a new heart in me.... Do not weary of patiently carrying me, a poor sinner, further. Oh if I could only

25

extinguish all the lusts of my flesh and be cleansed from my leprosy of sin by You. O Jesus, you Son of David, my Lord and God, have mercy on me.[2]

There was another confession in July.

Oh I wretched man: who will deliver me from this body of sin and death! Help me Oh my Jesus, purge all my sins according to your great mercy and give me a new better heart, a chaste, pure spirit, eager for truth and [desirous] of walking in your light...[3]

There were other moments of despair.

How anxious I am in my soul. Will the Lord forgive me my trespasses...[4]

Oh Lord Lord my heart is so cold and empty! Warm and revive it with your love to eternal life! Poor me—I preach repentance and forgiveness of sin to the people through the atoning death of Christ and my own heart longs for salvation. Oh Lord Jesus help me to achieve it.[5]

When will my frail body, like a perishable seed be laid in the ground! Oh Lord Jesus grant me the grace to be among those redeemed by your blood on the resurrection day. Oh if I could only totally belong to the Lord Jesus! Alarming doubts about the certainty of my salvation afflict my soul. Oh God how cold and disobedient my heart remains. Strive [my] soul that you enter the narrow gate of true repentance into eternal life.[6]

Today I celebrated my birthday. I have 48 years behind me. Oh how many a sin, how much treachery have I committed during my life. God forgive me all my sins, all my debts for the sake of the blood of Jesus Christ.[7]

Perhaps Jacob Epp's agony was simply a personal crisis of faith, a mid-life re-evaluation, or the "dark night of the soul" of which medieval mystics spoke. Or was it the widespread prevalence of disease and death in the settlement which always made life a serious affair? Then too there was the burden of public office. Here was Epp, the aging frustrated pastor, seeking to revitalize himself and his community. His personal quest for faith permeates his entire diary. What was it? How was it attained? Periods of doubt and penitential agony led to affirmations of faith, yet the process remained cyclical and lacking in firm assurance.

26

In the summer of 1837 David Epp complained that the light of the Gospel was "obscured in so many folk."[8] He wondered when the "dawn of true enlightenment" might begin to break. Were there other concerned voices and other prayers during the 1830s and 1840s? Church leaders with the exception of *Kleine Gemeinde* leaders, left no record of their longings and spiritual dreams. The prayers of David's son Jacob were equally fervent. "O gracious Lord and Savior. What will finally happen to us. Do not let us sink entirely into darkness and hopelessness."[9] A month later, distressed by the widespread sale of brandy he again pleaded: "If only help came from Zion and God redeemed his captive people."[10] Five years later Jacob still prayed for the salvation of his people. "Trusted Shepherd, save your flock which has strayed so far from you. Oh Lord have mercy."[11]

Some felt such prayers for renewal had been answered a few years earlier. In 1853 a young man in Neu-Kronsweide, Chortitza found peace with God after reading the sermons of the Wuerttemberg pietist Ludwig Hofacker. What was the nature of his inner experience? How did he inform others of his new found joy? Spontaneity apparently characterized both the young man's conversion and the revival which followed. The Chortitza region to which Neu-Kronsweide belonged was under the jurisdiction of elder Jacob Hildebrand. Later in the nineteenth century his son Cornelius, possibly utilizing family papers or recalling the stories told by his father, recounted the revival. In his words "one clearly felt the rustling of the wind concerning which Christ said to Nicodemus 'You know not whither it comes or where it goes.' "[12] The new movement "illumined the churches like the dawn of a new day."[13] The converts were serious pilgrims, and local villagers spoke of them as *die Frommen* (the pious ones) not in derision but in recognition of their godly walk.

Those with believing, longing hearts saw and rejoiced over it and thanked God in anticipation of a great glorious day. Father especially rejoiced with the newly converted, who so openly declared the assurance of forgiveness of sin in the blood of Jesus and hoped that these people would become the salt of the church and be a great blessing to it. He even viewed their initial, rather loudly expressed, joy in their newly experienced forgiveness as scriptural. At first he was kindly disposed to the movement and extended to it every sympathy and friendly good wishes.[14]

The beauty which Elder Hildebrand witnessed in the young movement was of short duration. An assertive minority was forcing its views upon an unwilling majority. Though the many tried to "distance themselves from the unwholesome activities,"[15] this proved difficult, as the leaders of the Neu-Kronsweide movement were "among these few and that cast a bad light upon the entire movement."[16] Johann Loewen of New-Kronsweide and Heinrich Hildebrandt of Burwalde apparently encouraged the dissenters to engage in an ongoing celebration of salvation. Their antics gradually eroded the elder's forbearance.

In the fall of 1855 Jacob Hildebrand was invited into the home of one of the non-conformists, the minister Peter Unrau. The meeting followed the regular worship service and was apparently called to facilitate discussion between the disputing parties. Both groups were still attending the services in the old church. A spirit of good will prevailed, for "much singing"[17] from the traditional hymnal interrupted the discourse.

The elder observed another scenario in the kitchen. In the words of Cornelius Hildebrand:

> The Unraus invited the meeting to stay for coffee. Since they had no children the female guests gave a helping hand. It became noticeable that Johann Loewen, the leader of the movement and a married man at that, found much to do in the kitchen and exchanged the "sister kiss" with the single sisters working there. Naturally father, who was very strict in ethical questions, could not reconcile this with the "new life," and his enthusiasm for the movement was considerably dampened. Even my mother and older brother observed incidents at this meeting that they could not reconcile with a pure Christian walk. Similarly, in the discussion with father a number of things came to the surface which signified a false concept of freedom, which permitted the use of the Spirit of God as a cover for the carnal satisfaction of impure lusts.[18]

Other episodes were equally painful for Hildebrand. At first the dissidents regularly attended worship services. The church began to fill, almost as if the old wanted something of the new. Such unity did not last. Not only were separate home worship services inaugurated but the "old order and its representatives"[19] were severely criticized. As the attack intensified, the old church became a place from which the pure in heart must flee. Key leaders left. When the Chortitza elder celebrated the Lord's Supper on the second Sunday after Pentecost in 1859 all his song leaders were absent. They were singing other melodies. Hildebrand's assistant and oldest fellow preacher did not participate. Finally Heinrich Neufeld, the son of the elder's old friend led the congregation in song. It seemed the disruption generated by the new faith would never end. Even this young song leader was rebaptized and joined the Molotschna dissenters in 1862. Members of Jakob Hildebrand's extended family were also affected. As Cornelius explained: "the cousins of my mother and at the same time our best friends went over to them."[20]

Hildebrand endured another kind of pain. Young Gerhard Wieler, following in the footsteps of his father Johann, began teaching in the village of Alt-Kronsweide. The year had hardly begun when local mothers, outraged over his new teaching methods, invaded the classroom. That very day the angry young teacher skated across the frozen Dnieper to protest this insult to his pedagogical dignity to Jakob Hildebrand. He won the support of an understanding elder. The village women beat a hasty retreat. No one tangled with Ohm Jakob.[21] A few years later the same Gerhard was in the home of the aged elder once more. It was not a friendly visit. The conversation had barely begun when Wieler, a zealous convert to the new movement, shouted: "You Ohm Jakob have preached many a soul into hell."[22] Hildebrand was unable to dampen the young man's ardor or broaden his tolerance. Ironically, by 1866 the same Gerhard was readmitted into the old church. Apparently he had not found the pure church among the separatists.[23]

The Neu-Kronsweide awakening of 1853-54 established an interesting sequence of response and counter response in the Chortitza settlement. Segments of the larger community tolerated and even welcomed the revival at first. Both traditionalists and reformers sat together on the same church benches. The Unrau house meeting attended by Hildebrand reflected a sense of togetherness characterized by dialogue, discussion and appeals to common sense. Moderation was still the order of the day. In the words of Cornelius Hildebrand:

> Father wished to unite, conciliate and hold together. He made many concessions to the movement, to the chagrin of some of his church members who wanted the elder to be firmer and harsher and often made sharp accusations because of his yielding attitude. Father, however, allowed

himself to be led by the heart rather than the mind and his Christian disposition was deeply afflicted by the split.[24]

In the end good will did not prevail. The religious revolution began to move towards the left. Doubts arose among the newly converted as to whether the old order provided adequate spiritual nurture. Was not traditional Mennonitism stagnant and corrupt? New kinds of leaders like the emotional Gerhard Wieler urged an end to compromise. They spoke loudly and demanded decisive action. Here were men inclined to the dramatic and heroic, men who desired a precise formula for the movement of God's Spirit in their midst. Their distinction between right and wrong, truth and falsehood allowed no compromise. They asserted that a few had found God, that many had not. Their dogmatic, doctrinaire stance intimidated the moderate majority. Toleration of a stagnant religious tradition was now out of the question. A saintly elder was upbraided for his inadequate preaching while the brothers and sisters of some months ago belonged to a "brothel."

The leaders of the Neu-Kronsweide awakening reacted against virtually every facet of the existing order. They rejected the old leadership, the old sermons, the old hymns and the old style of worship. All practices sanctified by custom and tradition were set aside. Within the old camp the harsh and intolerant responded in anger, the religiously sensitive in hurt and pain. By 1860 the Chortitza rebels had clearly separated from the Old Church. The pattern of future religious dissent was predictable. The average settler now associated revival with the breakup of the old order. He felt the advocates of the new salvation violated the prevailing community norms of orderliness and decency. Their behavior imprinted itself on the popular mind. Many felt their antics threatened the tranquility of the Mennonite world. Dissidents emerging elsewhere would receive a cold reception.

Elder Jakob Hildebrand was familiar with the "strong and resonant" voice of the South German preacher Eduard Wuest, who had visited Chortitza and on occasion corresponded with the elder. Wuest left his native Wuerttemberg in 1843 to serve the Neuhoffnungsthal congregation in Russia. It was a migrant group belonging to the so-called *Bruedergemeinde* which originated in Kornthal near Stuttgart in 1819. While still in the Wuerttemberg region this group was influenced by men like Johann Bengel (1687-1752) and Johann Hahn (1759-1819). Both men considered conversion and the life of sanctification as indispensable for a true, vital Christianity. They also subscribed to the practice of *Stunden* (conventicles), small group gatherings within a parish at which earnest seekers shared their mutual religious concerns. Bengel was also given to eschatological speculation. He regarded the book of Revelation as a precise outline of future events and boldly produced a chronology which set the second coming of Christ in 1836. The *Bruedergemeinde* migration to the Russian steppes was not unrelated to Bengel's millenialistic expectations which predicted Christ's second return in either Russia or Palestine. Internal strife among the settlers apparently prompted them to call Wuest. He was not the peacemaker they expected.

Records from Wuest's university days project an impetuous, robust young man who received at least three police citations for carousing and drunkenness.[25] This overflowing energy was directed to the service of religion following Wuest's dramatic conversion while a theology student. Lutheran authorities were soon investigating reports of crude language used during preaching services held in private homes and of *Stunden* lasting until midnight. Wuest's deviations were worse than suspected. He aroused "hate or love" in his preaching; he taught that custom was not an adequate reason for participating in the Lord's Supper; he demanded a decisive conversion; he failed to separate the sexes in his private meetings; he greeted people after the church service.[26] It seemed Wuest was a radical exponent of certain practices associated with Wuerttemberg piety in earlier decades. Christian Gottlob Pregizer (1751-1824) had insisted that a subjective emotionalism characterized by an assurance of sins forgiven and a profound continuous joy was a necessary proof of new life in Christ. Some groups within his circle exceeded his guidelines and held lively meetings which not only featured popularized hymn tunes accompanied by the zither, but ecstatic shouting as well.[27] Wuest may have been imitating Pregizer's style. Lutheran observers expressed concern about his excessive dramatics in the pulpit while a Wuerttemberg sympathizer urged him to "work more quietly."[28]

Little wonder that Wuest's first sermon in Russia shocked some of his listeners.[29] He spoke categorically of sin and grace, death and judgement, of Christ the Lamb who brought deliverance. Wuest apparently felt that many of his brothers on the steppes had succumbed to dead form and orthodoxy and needed to know the way of salvation. For the Wuerttemberg preacher the process involved a deep consciousness of sin and a dramatic struggle climaxing in an inner knowledge of divine

31

indwelling. The new birth was a decisive, overwhelming experience expressing itself in a continuous, deeply felt joy. Happiness soon became the mark of an authentic rebirth. For almost a decade the fervor of the Wuestian revivals was sustained by evangelistic preaching, fellowship meals featuring personal sharing and prayer as well as ecumenical mission festivals.

By 1852 Wuest rediscovered another aspect of his pietistic heritage—its concern with sanctification. He found that the more one celebrated salvation the more difficult it was to sustain its original vibrancy. The Cross not only brought joy to the repenting sinner but demanded discipleship from the newly created saint. Wuest found support for his new insights in the German periodical *Die Warte*, published by Christoff and Paulus Hoffmann. Those who still wished to celebrate grace accused Wuest and his church of strait-laced Pharisaism and dead ecclesiasticism. These so-called *Munteren* (joyful ones) now left Wuest's congregations. In the last years of his life Wuest confronted the recurring dilemma of pietism: the balance between experience and discipleship. An overemphasis on one produced superficiality while an unmitigated zeal for holiness catapulted the pilgrim back into the realm of law and orthodoxy against which he initially revolted. Wuest appears to have come in contact with the Chortitza dissidents shortly after their secession. He judged them harshly. In a letter to Elder Hildebrand dated September 28, 1854, he addressed the errors of the new movement.

> I have come to the conclusion, dear [friend], that the poor Kronsweide villagers, though I believe they have been awakened by God from death to life, have been permeated by a Satanic poison of false teaching and basic heresy. They themselves as well as the entire congregation [have become subject to this] because through their desperate, anti-Christian and blasphemous behavior, conversion generally and their own in particular has become suspect and the charge of the [spiritually] dead masses that conversion leads to insanity has some semblance of truth. You could hear references in my [Sunday] sermon to the blasphemous talk which I personally heard among the newly converted last Saturday. On Saturday Klassen opposed me with unmitigated gall and claimed that God cannot blame or condemn the individual. I heard similar teachings and expressions from Jakob Janzen and Loewen here in

Schoenwiese; as far as I know, the heresy, which has apparently been taken from Bohemian writings, emanates from Janzen.[30]

In his account Cornelius Hildebrand refers to "several human weaknesses" which the dissidents manifested "during their initial exuberant feelings of happiness."[31] Apparently there were those who "advanced the notion that the sins of the flesh were not imputed to a child of God."[32] This explicit reference to the idea that a person in a state of grace cannot sin probably explains Wuest's statement "that God cannot blame or condemn the individual." Wuest identified a Jakob Janzen as the originator of this unwholesome viewpoint so often associated with religious revival. Janzen was a minister in elder Hildebrand's congregation. Because of his heretical ideas he was forbidden to preach as early as 1852 and subsequently deposed. Cornelius Hildebrand still knew him as an honest if embittered Schoenwiese businessman in the early 1880s.[33]

Wuest's letter points to a second problem plaguing the young movement. He claimed they separated "the Spirit and the Word" for "behind the literal words of the Scriptures, they first seek the spiritual sense through the [Holy] Spirit dwelling in them.[34] Such an appeal to inner feeling and special enlightenment over and above the revealed Word contributed significantly to the instability of the non-conformists.

Meanwhile in the Molotschna settlement Wuest himself, thanks to his revivalist inclinations, was contributing to the beginnings of another religious secession. Some Mennonites from the city of Berdyansk were converted during Wuest's early ministry in that region. The shelling of Berdyansk during the Crimean War brought them to the Gnadenfeld region. A number of these had attended the so-called "brotherhood conferences" conducted by Wuest in his own parish and were also familiar with *Stunden*. The migrants introduced both practices to Gnadenfeld.[35] In his memoirs one of the participants, Jacob Bekker, notes that the conferences were held "every Saturday afternoon during full moon so that people from other villages could drive home in the moonlight."[36] Bekker also writes that he often "traveled together with Pastor Wuest in wagons loaded with people,"[37] en route to a missions conference. Apparently there was frequent contact between Wuest and this extension of his Berdyansk ministry.

More and more Mennonite names were gradually added to a

diffuse group of individuals known as the "Wuest brotherhood." They agreed with the content of Wuest's preaching and were attracted by the lively style of his meetings. In the Molotschna villages there were men like Heinrich Schmidt of Pastwa, Friedrich Lange of Gnadenfeld, Abraham Matthies of Rudnerweide, and the Gnadenfeld minister Nikolai Schmidt. In the city of Berdyansk Wuest counted Jakob Buhler and Leonhard Sudermann among his supporters. P.M. Friesen prints a long list of names associated with the Gnadenfeld congregation, all of whom belonged to the Wuest fraternity as late as 1858-1859.[38] Among these there were the "children of grace," Johann Claassen, Jakob Reimer and Wilhelm Bartel.[39] When visiting the Gnadenfeld area, Reimer's house usually served as Wuest's headquarters.[40]

At first Wuest's itinerant ministry placed him behind Mennonite pulpits. When this was forbidden by the elders he resorted to home visitation. In this setting there was Wuest the revivalist and preacher of free grace, Wuest the mission's advocate, and after 1850 Wuest the teacher of discipleship. Within the Gnadenfeld constituency Wuest's legacy remained intact until 1860.

Was it possible that while Wuest was preaching his followers sat too close to the front and were overwhelmed by his rich full voice? Were there not many Gnadenfeld brothers and sisters who, thanks to a long-standing pietistic heritage, already knew something of grace and justification? Maybe Wuest preached too categorically. His demand for a dramatic penitential agony climaxing in a secure knowledge of divine indwelling and continuous joy possibly made the older Gnadenfeld piety, though very similar in form, appear a trifle obsolete.

Later oral tradition affirmed that Wuest's preaching brought Lutherans, Mennonites and Wuerttembergers together in Gnadenfeld not only for fellowship but also for communion celebrations. By 1860 ecclesiastical authorities no longer tolerated such practices. Communion participation was not only limited to Gnadenfeld church members but accompanied by the sacrosanct notion that it could only be administered by church leaders. Wuest's Mennonite disciples apparently desired more frequent communion and even suggested it be held in various homes. Some believed the service should not include those members of the community whose religious commitment was nominal at best. Both sensitivities probably formed the background of a private communion held in Elisabethal during the fall of 1859. It was not an impetuous or rebellious act. In their quest for inner peace they had endured an agonizing struggle for the assurance of salvation. They were also deeply convinced of the need for a Christian walk in which faith was expressed in everyday life. The 1859 communicants had also concluded that the Lord's Supper must not be shared with those of nominal faith or those lacking in serious discipleship. On the one hand their action stemmed from a strong inner conviction, on the other it was necessitated by Elder August Lenzmann, who, had earlier refused to serve communion separately or more frequently.

By rejecting the old piety the dissidents found themselves in a religious, cultural and intellectual vacuum. Celebrating communion proved to be a dangerous, destabilizing move. The blueprint for a new religious direction now depended on the vitality of the inner journey or upon outside models. Wuest's ministry provided a good measure of both. Initially he advocated the new life experience as the only measure of true spirituality. Then, after 1850, he promoted the need for sanctification with equal vigor. The Molotschna nonconformists advocated both extremes of the Wuestian formula: the vigorous pursuit of discipleship with its demand for a pure, separated church and the equally vigorous celebration of the ecstacy of the inner life. The resulting extremes of severity and frivolity, sobriety and intemperance, moderation and excess made their subsequent story both distasteful and exciting.

NOTES

[1] David Epp Diary (Mennonite Heritage Centre, Winnipeg, Manitoba), December 31, 1841

[2] Jacob Epp Diary (Mennonite Heritage Centre, Winnipeg, Manitoba), June 18, 1868.

[3] *Ibid.*, July 18, 1868

[4] September 7, 1868

[5] September 22, 1868

[6] September 25, 1868

[7] December 26, 1868

[8] David Epp Diary, July 15, 1837

[9] Jacob Epp Diary, January 18, 1860

[10] February 23, 1860

[11] December 28, 1865

[12] The original account was preserved thanks to publication in a Russian Mennonite periodical. See Cornelius Hildebrand, "Aus der Kronsweider Erweckungszeit," *Der Botschafter*, VIII (1913), nos. 6, 8-19. It and other

documents are translated in John B. Toews, "The Early Mennonite Brethren: Some Outside Views," *Mennonite Quarterly Review*, Vol. LVIII, no. 2 (April, 1984), 83-124.

13 Toews, 96
14 *Ibid.*
15 *Ibid.*, 98
16 *Ibid.*
17 *Ibid.*, 99
18 *Ibid.*
19 *Ibid.*
20 *Ibid.*, 100
21 *Ibid.*, 107-109
22 *Ibid.*, 110
23 *Ibid.*, 111
24 *Ibid.*, 98
25 Victor G. Doerksen, "Kirchliche Verwuestung? Eduard Hugo Otto Wuest in Wuerttemberg, 1844/45" (Paper presented to the Symposium on Russian Mennonite History, Winnipeg, Manitoba, 1977). Doerksen discovered some primary material in the Landeskirchliches Archiv (Stuttgart) under Akte A27, Volume 3632. The material fills significant gaps in our knowledge of Wuest's early career (1841-1847). It suggests that his preaching, both as to style and content, crystalized before he left to minister to the German colonies in Russia.
26 Ibid., 10-15
27 See Gotthold Muller, *Christian Gottlob Pregizer. Biographie und Nachlass* (Stuttgart, 1962)
28 Doerksen, 16
29 P.M. Friesen, *Die Alt-Evangelische Mennonitische Bruederschaft in Russland* (Halbstadt, Taurien, 1911), 175-182
30 Eduard Wuest to Jakob Hildebrand, Schoenwiese, September 28, 1854. Toews, 112.
31 *Ibid.*, 97
32 *Ibid.*
33 *Ibid.*, 113
34 *Ibid.*, 112
35 According to his biographer Wuest felt a close spiritual kinship with the Mennonites. See Jakob Prinz, *Die Kolonien der Bruedergemeinde. Ein Beitrag zur Geschichte der deutschen Kolonien in Suedrussland* (Moscow, 1898), p. 86ff.
36 Jacob Bekker, *Origin of the Mennonite Brethren Church* (Hillsboro, Kansas, 1973), 26
37 *Ibid.*, 27
38 Friesen, 104
39 Friesen, 225
40 *Ibid.*, 224

CHAPTER IV
DANGEROUS JOURNEY

The Mennonites belonging to the Wuest "brotherhood" at first had no intentions of leaving the church in which they were raised. Instead they demanded that the old piety accommodate their special religious sensitivities. They wanted a believers' church based on a voluntary membership which stood within Mennonitism but which did not include the entire community. However pious their intentions, the action of these non-conformists slighted many Gnadenfeld brothers and sisters. There were widespread demands for the excommunication of the radicals. The private communion soon generated vigorous debate during two Gnadenfeld church meetings. A vocal, protesting minority forced the elder's hand and demanded the dissenters leave the church. They did. The break with the old order came suddenly and unexpectedly. Had the reformers pushed too hard or had orthodoxy become too brittle? These were mute questions. The debate was closed; the dialogue ended.

It was now clear that a spiritual pilgrimage in the context of the traditional community was impossible. The eighteen Molotschna villagers who seceded January 6, 1860, felt they had no other option. Not all the signatories were members of the Gnadenfeld congregation nor was the impetuous response to a stormy congregational meeting necessarily indicative of the dynamic which gave birth to the new movement. The action of the majority of the dissidents was probably rooted in their personal, protracted spiritual journeys. They were sure of their new life experience and certain of the direction in which they were travelling. In their secession statement and in letters addressed to the leaders of the Old Church they sought to articulate their religious concerns.

The tone of the secession manifesto was overwhelmingly negative.[2] The first sentence focused on the corruption of contemporary Mennonitism. The purity of the believers' church could not be sustained amidst such decadence and therefore "we herewith are completely severing ourselves from the corrupt church." Generally the document reaffirmed the traditional Mennonite confession of faith. The dissenters cited their views on baptism, the Lord's Supper, feet washing, the election of ministers and the ban. Baptism must be "ministered upon a true, living faith." Communion fellowship with the carnally-minded was contrary to Scripture. The ordinance was "not an emblem of fellowship of believers with unbelievers." As such they could not associate with "lovers of money, drunkards and blasphemers." Church discipline was essential and all "willful sinners must be excommunicated from the fellowship of believers." The proclamation's dominant theme focused on the purity of the church. It could not, they insisted, include the entire community and was not necessarily represented by contemporary institutions and leaders. The document made no mention of re-baptism or immersion baptism.

When the Ohrloff elder Johann Harder reported on his discussions with the radicals he made reference to a written statement in which they declared that "each would have preferred to remain a member of his own church" but because "ministers do not regulate matters according to the Word of God" could not do so.[3] In a letter to the Ohrloff-Halbstadt church council they explained that they did not view their community "as one having degenerated into a complete devil's service" and had only withdrawn from "the corrupt churches" not the brotherhood.[4] They celebrated the Lord's Supper apart "because we could not in good conscience observe it with unbelievers."[5]

Since the Old Church was deeply interwoven with the fabric of society the demand for a new order threatened a delicate, long-standing balance within the Mennonite world. Though the secessionists asserted that their beliefs were "in full accord with our beloved Menno Simons" they failed to realize the tremendous social and political implications of their demands. In a sense they were repeating an old Anabaptist theme. Radical religion spawned a new group desirous of putting its new values into practice. This necessitated the rejection of the old piety and the creation of a new peoplehood.

The vigor of the protest ensured confrontation rather than conciliation from the very outset. The old piety felt compelled to protect itself. The majority of elders, secure in their alliance with the Mennonite state, moved against the nonconformists. The struggle for the fledgling movement now centered on the retention of their legal status as Mennonites. The preoccupation with the inner journey which had spawned their initial nonconformity seemed less important. As in Luther's day an ecclesiastical institution embracing all of society and following an ancient and sacrosanct creed soon forced the secessionists to define their protest and articulate their theology. Such pressure basically squelched the potential of their religious revolution. By committing their ideas to paper in letters and official declarations the dissidents formalized their spiritual journey while it was still in its infancy. The ideas and experiences contributing to their liberation became less evolving and dynamic. In a sense they replaced a gospel with a creed. The secession document was almost a preamble to a confession of faith: a nonconformity born out of a dynamic renewal institutionalized prematurely.

The legal-bureaucratic confrontation at an early stage of the Brethren secession not only narrowed the scope of the spiritual quest but terminated further dialogue. In its absence the larger community remained ignorant of the reformers' concerns. As hearsay replaced open communication it constructed its own image of the dissidents in the public mind. Meanwhile a few protagonists generated a series of administrative documents in which the minority proclaimed its innocence and cried persecution while orthodox leaders expressed concern about the collapse of the old order caused by seditious religious attitudes and practices.

The protesters now stood alone. They were no longer a part of the old *Bruederschaft* (brotherhood). In part their new sense of identity was forged by the rejection of the larger community. They had only each other. There was also a common memory— some had once belonged to the "Wuest brotherhood." Here was a continuation of those ideals. After all the German language connotation of "brother" was especially intimate. Where was its meaning more significant and more applicable than in a new church of the truly committed? Little wonder that the dissidents soon spoke of themselves as *die Brueder* (the Brethren). It would be some time before others in the community used the term so positively.

Brethren dissent was not only a search for revitalized religion but a quest for a broader world view *(Weltanschauung)* as well. By reading the books and periodicals of spiritually akin groups in Germany the dissidents broadened their cultural-intellectual horizons. As Christian pilgrims, they looked west for their nurture. In the process of fulfilling their religious aspirations they not only affirmed German as their primary devotional language but absorbed some of the cross currents in contemporary German theology. In this context the Brethren were subjected to pietist and baptist influences which frequently related religious vitality to an ongoing, subjective religious experience.

Was the Brethren protest also a revolution of the poor? Could the landless now find a religious outlet for their frustration? Did they use the prevailing dissent as a means of curbing the power of the wealthy and influential? Unfortunately no surviving registers clearly designate occupations of the early Brethren. Some inferences can be made from other sources. The radicals mentioned in Jacob Epp's diary were ordinary farmers like himself. Men like Johann and Gerhard Wieler, whatever their emotional inclinations, obviously belonged to a fledgling Mennonite intelligentsia. As a young teacher Gerhard confidently engaged elder Hildebrand in religious dialogue while his brother Johann eventually became the president of the Russian Baptist Conference in 1884. Likewise Elder Abraham Unger's connection with the Baptist Johann Oncken suggests an intellectual-religious awareness well beyond the village context.

A similar diversity characterized the dissidents in the Molotschna. Jacob Bekker in his uncontrived, straightforward manner, speaks of the Russian servant girl in Gnadenheim who helped convert the local pub owner,[6] "Herman Peters the drummaker"[7] (who was really a carpenter), and of a landlord converted in a prayer meeting in the Saratov area.[8] There was also the Gnadenfeld minister, "the wealthiest materially"[9] who initially sympathized with the nonconformists, and Johann Claassen who bought a "closed model carriage"[10] to go to Kharkov at what seemed to be a moment's notice. Other early adherents included school teachers not identified by name[11] and the shopkeeper Jakob Mathies whose wife, angered by Bekker's piety, physically attacked him.[12] Still others who later migrated to the Kuban belonged to the "poorer and the poor."[13] The opening of a new frontier naturally attracted the landless or those who felt they were persecuted.

There are some other things which can be known about the early dissidents such as their family connections,[14] church affiliation, residence and occupations.[15] Many apparently belonged to a landless intelligentsia. Unfortunately there are many things which will never be known. How many were there who agreed with the signatories, but for personal, congregational, family or even economic reasons refrained from taking a decisive stance? Who, amid the varieties of humankind in Chortitza and the Molotschna were the true seekers or the merely curious, the deeply committed or the momentarily ecstatic? And what of those who claimed new life and personal salvation but lacked a structural framework, a formal theology or even a vocabulary in which to place their experience? Should they seek refuge within the old, which remained inflexible, or the new, which was steadily in flux? In such circumstances they possibly remained silent and withdrawn. For many the rapidly changing political and religious circumstances allowed no time for calm reflection or prolonged neutrality. There was no middle ground.

Thanks to the caprice of events and personalities the early Brethren stood alone. A combative argumentative stance on the one hand and a silence interrupted only by official actions and documents on the other, left one side isolated and vulnerable, the other hurt and increasingly hostile. Since old worship patterns and songs of faith were associated with orthodoxy and meaningless religious form, the mode of religious expression was now determined by the inner ecstacy associated with spiritual rebirth. It was time to shout for joy. In Chortitza the celebration of salvation emerged gradually. For a time the dissidents attended worship services in the old church and invited their elder to house services for dialogue and discussion. On such occasions they still sang from the old hymnal. There was no dramatic exodus, only a drawn-out process of separation. There is little information on the ongoing celebrations of the Neu-Kronsweide revivalists. Cornelius Hildebrand's account essentially reflects the evolving antagonism between old and new as well as the dissident's tendency towards doctrinal heresy. He nevertheless refers to their "rather loudly expressed joy in their newly experienced forgiveness,"[16] "their initial exuberant feelings of happiness,"[17] and the fact that "they sang and jumped, beat on boxes and chests on which they placed pots and cutlery to increase the noise."[18]

Accounts of the exuberance movement in the Molotschna are more numerous and explicit. P.M. Friesen relates how Jacob Reimer, in a letter of 1861, described a lively Sunday at Jakob Reimer's house in Gnadenfeld when "the Brethren leaped and danced."[19] Reimer, in a probable reference to this episode, subsequently informed Johann Claassen in St. Petersburg that he could "no longer tolerate such bedlam in my home as took place last Sunday."[20] A few days later Johann's wife Katherina informed him of a Pentecost service in an abandoned mosque where "several leaped and danced, some played and sang, and then almost all shouted for joy."[21] Somewhat later when the radicals had excommunicated the moderate Brethren, things went from bad to worse. Records cited by Friesen speak of "uninhibited sound and fury"[22] of dancing "until they were soaked with perspiration,"[23] of meetings at which "they did not allow any sermons."[24] During the so-called June reforms of 1865 specific reference was made to "wild expressions of joy" which consisted of "dancing"[25] and "frenzy and dancing."[26]

In his memoirs Jacob Bekker elaborates on the 1861 Pentecost service held in the empty mosque. The participants became so zealous and enthusiastic that they shouted for joy, jumped and leaped, which in turn elicited approving responses from others shouting "Hallelujah! Victory! Glory! Amen! May the Lord grant it."[27] He further relates how he sought to subdue this ecstacy on three separate occasions during the meeting by reading Psalms.[28] Bekker also provides a unique list of musical instruments used by the early Brethren: organs, flutes, violins, guitars and musical triangles. He also mentions the use of the vigorously beaten drum confiscated by the village mayor only to reappear in a second edition.[29]

Heinrich Janzen reports his encounters with the Molotschna extremists in his personal recollections. In one scenario he relates how hymns sung according to different folk melodies were accompanied by wild dancing and jumping.

> They clutched their hands at the air as if they wanted to snatch the object of their joy. Suddenly they stopped in order to pray one after the other, or better to thank God for his work of grace on their behalf. When the words of any one supplicant seemed particularly appropriate they suddenly shouted loudly once again and pursued other like practices. Through such activity they gradually forfeited the name *Frommen* and were now called *Froehliche* (the Happy), *Hupfer* (Jumpers) and *Springer* (Leapers), designations which were now more appropriate.[30]

In another setting he observed two men sitting on a bench facing each other. A hymn sung according to a street melody generated a lively rhythm. Before long the bench became a wooden horse prancing back and forth across the floor in time to the music.[31]

How can the exuberance movement in early Brethren history be explained? One answer might point to a rigid, brittle society ripe for revolution. Religious discontent had reached a breaking point, the predictable explosion could not be restrained. Mennonite religion was so joyless and straight-laced that some excitement was essential. Exuberance was a necessary emotional outlet in the face of an unyielding orthodoxy. Another approach might argue it was a fringe movement spearheaded by a few radical leaders. The position is difficult to sustain in view of the fact that moderates like Johann Claassen and Jacob Reimer at first participated in the practice. Old Church adherents, possibly overwhelmed by the sensational character of their worship services, remembered most Brethren as celebrants. Portraying the phenomenon as a momentary digression or flash in the pan further distorts the historical facts. Excessive celebrations began as early as 1854 and continued as late as 1865. They were demonstrative, occasionally public, and at times clearly out of control. The body too was not beyond manifesting some of its aspirations. The movement was not an extreme charismatic manifestation. There was no focus on the work and role of the Holy Spirit nor any stated desire for a special filling of the Spirit.

Collective memories associated with the style of Eduard Wuest's piety must have provided a model for the Brethren new life experience. Wuest made much of both the penitential struggle and the joy associated with the attainment of faith. Profoundly felt emotions not only played a part in the search for peace but tended to become the mark of true faith after conversion. The temptation to recreate both catharsis and ecstasy was overwhelming. None of the early Brethren had been on this pathway previously. Quite naturally they were reluctant to move faith beyond feeling. Like the early Wuest they preferred the emotional enjoyment of religion to the ardent demands of discipleship. Then, too, Wuest arrived on the Russian steppes singing and his Mennonite disciples loved his melodies. Perhaps the situation was akin to periodic revival manifestations where music played a critical role in shaping the inner quality of religious experience. As the drums beat louder and increased in tempo some of the Brethren moved left of this Wuestian legacy. Tender spiritual insights associated with new beginnings and new songs were trampled or drowned out in the shouting and jumping which followed.[32]

The diary of Jacob Epp reflects another dimension. On April 15, 1862 he was visited by a neighbor who informed him "that no one in [our] church would be saved if he did not leave it... Redekopp told me directly that I was not converted."[33] Some three years later he reported on a visit with an Aaron Lepp. "We discussed his exodus and that of his coreligionists. He still calls our church a whore and [affirms] that he and his consorts are on the right pathway."[34] In the course of the Neu-Kronsweide revival, according to Cornelius Hildebrand, the dissidents "called the church a brothel"[35] and "wanted nothing more to do with the unconverted as they called members of the Old Church."[36]

Such a determined rejection of every facet of the established piety ensured the loss of traditional worship patterns, church polity and hymnody. Spiritual destabilization among the Chortitza and Molotschna dissidents only intensified after the break with the old order. The revolution moved too fast and too far to the left. By cutting all ties with what had been, the nonconformists found themselves in the wilderness. Before long a lunatic fringe burned the very materials which nurtured their initial quest for new life. In the words of Heinrich Epp:

> Gerhard Wieler stepped before the congregation, held the Bible high and shouted: "This book, the Bible, is the only book which shows us the way to salvation. All other books cannot help in this regard and must therefore be destroyed and burned according to Acts 19:19" Many were led astray and burned their books.[37]

They had destroyed even their recent past. As a group devoid of any tradition or sense of history they became vulnerable to every excess. Soon arrogant and inexperienced leaders, given to rhetoric and narrow dogma, proclaimed the exclusiveness of the new faith and the total failure of the Old Church. Unfettered by religious tradition and practice some claimed the direct inspiration of the Holy Spirit as they boldly proclaimed a new order.

Despising all accumulated wisdom they engaged in literalistic interpretation of Scripture, interpretations which frequently justified their excesses. Heinrich Janzen recalled the Bible studies in which he had participated.

> What both struck and angered me about the Bible studies was the caprice with which a number of participants

interpreted certain Scripture passages. For example, in the opinion of one of Cl.'s grown sons, of all the animals on earth horses would probably get to heaven because some Scriptures indicate that there were horses in heaven. Another view held by the majority of Bible study participants was that all non-Christians, including innocent little children, went to hell because they lacked the saving faith in Jesus. I was not pleased that horses went to heaven and small children to hell...[38]

P.M. Friesen observed that the radical Brethren "read the Word of God selectively"[39] and were therefore able to justify the excesses associated with their services. In an 1854 letter to elder Hildebrand, Eduard Wuest gave his assessment of the earlier extremists in Chortitza.

> In the main these people are impregnated with their heresy through their method of scriptural exposition. Behind the literal words of the Scriptures they first seek the spiritual sense through the [Holy] Spirit dwelling in them ... Separating the Spirit and the Word as they do is contrary to all Reformation principles of scripture exposition and opens the door to all error and all nonsense.[40]

Were the revivalists in the Molotschna now making the same error? The bizarre and pathetic scenes of wild celebration which so marred early Brethren history were mainly rooted in the radical nature of the separation from the Old Church. Memories of the early Wuest celebrating grace helped fill this vacuum. Spontaneous innovation loosely invoking scriptural authority occupied the remaining space. Under such circumstances it was impossible to develop a broad-based theology regulating the new life. There was only the repeated celebration of the initial religious experience. The young movement faced a formidable challenge. Some had shouted and danced. It was a dramatic performance and many remembered only that. Most forgot about the quietistic Brethren who abhorred spiritual violence.

NOTES

1 P.M. Friesen, *Die Alt-Evangelische Mennonitische Bruederschaft in Russland 1789-1910* (Halbstadt, Taurien, 1911), 186-188.
2 *Ibid.*, 189-192.
3 Jacob P. Bekker, *Origin of the Mennonite Brethren Church* (Hillsboro, Kansas, 1973), 62.

4 *Ibid.*, 10.
5 *Ibid.*
6 *Ibid.*, 100-101.
7 *Ibid.*, 84-85.
8 *Ibid.*, 36-37.
9 *Ibid.*, 27.
10 *Ibid.*, 82.
11 *Ibid.*, 96-97, 101. Two of these signed the secession document. *Ibid.*, 80.
12 *Ibid.*, 96-97.
13 Heinrich Friesen and Cornelius P. Toews, *Die Kubaner Ansiedlung* (Steinbach, Manitoba, 1953), 17.
14 Alan Peters, "Brotherhood and Family: Implications of Kinship in Mennonite Brethren History," in Abraham Friesen (ed.), *P.M. Friesen and His History: Understanding Mennonite Brethren Beginnings* (No. 2 of Perspectives on Mennonite Life and Thought, Fresno, California, Center for Mennonite Brethren Studies, 1979), 35-50.
15 James Urry, "A Religious or Social Elite? The Mennonite Brethren in Imperial Russia," Symposium on Dynamics of Faith and Culture in Mennonite Brethren History, Winnipeg, Canada, November 14-15, 1986, pp. 26ff.
16 J.B. Toews, "The Early Mennonite Brethren: Some Outside Views," *Mennonite Quarterly Review*, LVIII (1984), no. 2, 96.
17 *Ibid.*, 97.
18 *Ibid.*, 100.
19 Friesen, 224-25.
20 *Ibid.*
21 *Ibid.*, 225.
22 *Ibid.*, 279.
23 *Ibid.*, 280.
24 *Ibid.*
25 *Ibid.*, 234.
26 *Ibid.*, 280.
27 Bekker, 84.
28 *Ibid.*, 85.
29 *Ibid.*, 84.
30 Toews, 118.
31 *Ibid.*, 120-121.
32 See Harry Loewen, "Echoes of Drumbeats: The Movement of Exuberance Among the Mennonite Brethren," *Journal of Mennonite Studies*, vol. 3 (1985), 118-127.
33 Jakob Epp Diary (Mennonite Heritage Centre, Winnipeg, Manitoba), April 15, 1862.
34 *Ibid.*, April 30, 1865.
35 Toews, 98.
36 *Ibid.*, 100.
37 Heinrich Epp, *Notizen aus dem Leben und Wirken des verstorbenen Aeltesten Abraham Unger* (Halbstadt, 1907), 14.
38 Toews, 119.
39 Friesen, 279.
40 Toews, 112-113

CHAPTER V
BECOMING GOD'S PEOPLE

Several years of dancing and shouting brought exhaustion. The heroic energy dedicated to reform and the creation of a new order was spent. The experiental pendulum, which had swung as far left as possible, began its counter stroke. Amid all the ecstasy and noise, novel religious modes had emerged. There was a new style of preaching, a new form of baptism and a new pattern of worship. There were also new songs. As the search for stabilization began, the demands for normalcy in all these areas intensified. Sincere repentance culminated in the so-called "June Reforms" of 1865, which among other things unanimously declared that "the wild expressions of joy, such as dancing," were not pleasing to God.[1] The moderates, so abused by the early radicals, were again in control. In 1872 the young movement convened its first general conference: now the will of the many, not the few, would prevail. The task which confronted the Brethren was formidable. If they were to become God's people they would have to solve the dilemma which so marred Wuest's ministry—the balance between a Christian experience which felt good and a discipleship which demanded more than emotion. Survival depended on the moderates. They had to transform a reckless, individualistic emotionalism into a sober yet vital piety capable of sustaining and spanning successive generations. From that perspective the accomplishments after 1870 far surpassed those of the previous decade.

In most instances the early celebrations of joy, however excessive they may have been, reflected a genuine conversion. Unfortunately, the documentation left by P.M. Friesen contains few "conversion stories" of either laity or leaders, though the Brethren belief in the necessity of the new birth is clearly portrayed. The little we know about early Brethren conversions suggests that they set few pre-conditions for their spiritual quest. The processes associated with their new life experiences were therefore rather diverse. Conversion was predominantly an adult affair and as such an often agonizing, lengthy journey. Men and women in mid-life or even advanced age believed and were baptized.

Surviving conversion accounts of the 1880s and 1890s provide the only clues to the inner pattern of the spiritual pilgrimages of the 1850s and 1860s. The memoranda of these second or even third generation Brethren heirs may well have been subject to some standardization. After all, the search for a descriptive vocabulary capable of defining and describing the various categories of the subjective experience had been underway for several decades. Furthermore the concept of conversion became an important reference point in determining eligibility for church membership. Members of the congregation had to be satisfied that the pattern of personal salvation was akin to their own. In such a setting ideas associated with conversion may, in contrast to the earlier decades, have become subject to greater conformity. As it developed, this language of the inner experience not only provided a point of contact with the mindset of the founding fathers but became an influential factor in determining the style of Brethren piety.

What were some of the elements in the Brethren profile of conversion during the last two decades of the nineteenth century? All the accounts reflect a sense of deep personal sinfulness which usually derived from specific transgressions. Smoking and drinking, common practices in the Russian Mennonite world of that day, were frequently cited as key transgressions.[2] Some mentioned the sins committed while in "worldly company"[3] while others confessed to "worldly pursuits at weddings."[4] Drinking, smoking, card playing and obscene talk were the cardinal evils associated with such occasions. These shortcomings were longstanding. David Epp listed them in the 1840s as did his son Jacob in the 1860s. Some Brethren converts identified very specific issues. One recalled how he smoked and read Hofacker's sermons,[5] while another acknowledged his obsession with reading romances.[6]

When describing their crisis experience the Brethren often used words like *Suendennot* (a profound sense of sinfulness) or *Seelenangst* (mental anguish).[7] There was a feeling of inadequacy and shortcoming, despondency and hopelessness. The search for peace was usually a protracted one lasting days, weeks and even months. Recounting his own conversion in the summer of 1896 the later emigration leader B.B. Janz spoke of his "struggle for forgiveness" which involved repeated prayers of "confession and self-surrender" yet there was "no response from above."[8] Similarly the preacher and teacher A.H. Unruh engaged in a lengthy search for salvation[9] as did the itinerant minister and later elder Herman Neufeld.[10] In this struggle for true faith there was a striving for a genuine "breakthrough"[11] and a preoccupation with becoming joyful (*froh werden*) and being joyful (*froh sein*).[12] When the individual finally secured assurance of salvation (*Heilsgewissheit*) a public prayer of thanksgiving became symbolic of the new commitment.[13]

The trauma associated with the new birth became a constant reference point in the practice of everyday Brethren piety. Herman Neufeld left an interesting description of prayer week activities in his local church.

> For our congregation in Nikolayevka in the Ignatyevo settlement Christmas was the best time of the year for the spiritual life of our congregation. Many were led to repentance during that period. This was also the case during the prayer week of the 1904 Christmas period.
>
> We held the prayer week in the following manner. We brothers and sisters and many others gathered every evening. After one or two songs were sung we opened with Scripture reading and prayer. Then a number who desired to do so prayed alternately. Various brothers and sisters related their conversion. More prayers and testimonies followed. Songs or [single] verses of songs were sung in between. The Lord manifested himself and blessed the prayers and the testimonies so that tears were shed and many were [inwardly] moved. It seemed that souls wished to repent and be converted and we had a blessed time.[14]

Here was a portrait of a meeting style which the Brethren practiced for decades. How did this setting, with its prayers, songs, tears and recounting of conversion relate to becoming a people of God? It was a lay piety stressing the experiental and personal. These gatherings, varying little in format, were regularly held throughout the Brethren constituency. They offer an explanation of the movement's steady growth during the nineteenth century, both on the frontiers and in the established settlements.

The portraits of church life left by late nineteenth century accounts appear almost too idyllic. Brethren house or school meetings encouraged warm and intimate fellowship. When reporting these occasions, participants often spoke of the *selige Stunden* (blessed hours) which they had spent together. Ordinary church members were broadening their understanding of faith theologically and caring for each other. There was openness, vulnerability, and authenticity. Genuine concern and empathy also meant evangelism. Conversion accounts frequently reflect the relational qualities which attracted the seeker to the Brethren. Counsel and reassurance was easy to find in such a non-threatening environment. One did not have to search for community after conversion. Care-givers and care-receivers were linked together from the very outset. There was also little difficulty in accommodating children and young adults in such a setting.

This congregational style held an additional benefit. The pursuit of holiness and sanctification occurred in the midst of the congregation. Small group interaction easily connected faith with everyday problems. Discipleship became a response to the ebb and flow of life experience. The results were gratifying. Holiness was corporately, not individually defined. It was difficult for dominant personalities to impose narrow definitions of piety upon a participatory church democracy. Further, the situation allowed neither the formalization of a dogmatic theology nor the pursuit of mystical ecstasy. The inner life, however radiant and glorious, found its outlet in obligation to the larger community. Individuals inclined towards spiritual pretense and artificiality or a public display of their piety might find the congregation probing the vitality of their personal pilgrimage. The Brethren "house church" necessarily generated an existential theology.

There was another practice which helped to solidify the Brethren—the itinerant ministry. The first conference held in 1872 elected five itinerant preachers. Their task: to contact and nurture all the scattered Brethren adherents. Their agenda of activity soon included home visitation, conducting meetings and Bible studies in schools and private residences, and participation in large assemblies at mission and thanksgiving festivals. It was an effective strategy designed to overcome the problems of a minority movement scattered throughout Russia.

In some villages the Brethren consisted of only a few families. In 1891 Jacob Fast met with six adults and some children in Blumstein, Wilhelm Loewen spoke to a house meeting of twenty persons in Tiegerweide, while Heinrich Friesen thought it worthwhile to visit a remote village where only seven families lived.[15] Even well established congregations were small. In 1894 the Sparrau Mennonite Brethren Church consisted of only 32 members[16] while the Margenau congregation numbered 73.[17] In the same year the minister, David Duerksen, reported that there were only 48 Brethren families in the entire Ufa settlement.[18] Services in private homes or schools nurtured these small groups of believers and for decades constituted a modest but effective mode of evangelism.

The carefully planned schedules of some five or six traveling ministers ensured annual contact with virtually all adherents. Such activity was crucial. Brethren emergence and growth coincided with the establishment of new Mennonite settlements throughout European Russia. The young church was naturally involved in this dispersion process and the new frontiers threatened its cohesiveness. The itinerant ministry constituted a realistic response to the crisis. Dedicated men, usually working for meager salaries, sequentially visited all congre-gations. By their cultivation of personal and public religion they generated a steady reaffirmation of a distinct Brethren identity. The ministry created a sense of the common faith and established uniform practices in worship and liturgy. It produced a strong sense of belonging, even in small, remote communities.

Some indication of how well the itinerant ministers served the Brethren constituency with their home visitations, Bible studies and preaching services can be found in their annual reports.[19] Early in 1890 Wilhelm Loewen reported that he had travelled in the Molotschna Colony for 49 days, made 202 home visitations and preached 30 sermons.[20] Four years later David Duerksen reported that in 41 days of travel he had covered 4,908 versts by train and 500 versts by wagon. He had held 57 services and visited 80 homes.[21] A traveling minister was frequently appointed for a two or four month period. Particular attention was paid to new settlements. Hermann Neufeld travelled through two colonies during January and February, 1890, visiting 60 homes and preaching 30 sermons.[22] During the 1895-96 season he travelled for 145 days, preached 126 times and visited 200 homes.[23] After ten years he estimated he had travelled over 100,000 verst by train, covered 3,000 verst by wagon, preached 3,000 times, and entered some 3,000 homes. He had visited virtually every village in all of the settlements where Brethren were present.[24] Later in life Neufeld reflected on his thirty-eight years as an itinerant minister. When he compiled his meticulously kept records he discovered he had preached 5,000 sermons, conducted c. 2,000 Bible Studies, made 6,000 house visitations and travelled in the vicinity of 300,000 versts by rail, steamship, and wagon. When it came to baptisms, communion services funerals and marriages his records were less precise. Neufeld estimated that he had conducted approximately 500 of each.[25]

The effectiveness of the itinerant ministry was enhanced by the so-called *Missionsschule* (mission school) or *Bibelkursus* (Bible course). These sessions, which began as early as 1875 and were regularly held by the 1890s, were open to ministers and interested laity. They lasted a few days, weeks or even months. The courses not only provided inspiration and preaching content for local lay ministers but ensured greater Bible knowledge for the rank and file in the local congregation. In 1893, for example, Jakob Reimer conducted a Bible course in Gnadenheim, Molotschna, which was followed by a three week seminar in language study and orthography for lay ministers by the prominent Mennonite educator Cornelius Unruh.[26] During the winter of 1894 the Baptist, Ivan W. Kargel from St. Petersburg, conducted another course in Andreasfeld.[27]

The importance of such training was clearly demonstrated in the case of Herman Neufeld who began participating in such courses as early as 1888, the year of his ordination. Such yearly sessions (in addition to private reading and study) constituted the only formal ministerial training this Brethren elder ever obtained.[28]

There were several other activities designed to enhance the Brethren sense of peoplehood. Most churches not only conducted regular Sunday Schools but organized associations of young men and women as well. There were at least two other activities sustaining congregational vitality—the ladies mission circle and the choir. In a broader context the emergence of the *Saengerfest* (Song Festival) in the 1890s supplemented the overall sense of community.

Songs, missions and thanksgiving festivals, Bible studies, home visitations, village school meetings, regular ministerial visits, common sermon styles—all contributed towards a religious uniformity which generated its own peoplehood.

Conversion, both as to process and inner meaning, was clearly defined. *Bekehrung* remained crucial to the Brethren sense of identity and well being and continued to be expounded and experienced. Yet the celebration of salvation was not an end in itself but took place in a setting sensitive to the demands of discipleship. The inner dynamics of the community focused on the nurture of the new Christian, on mutual caring and admonishment and on the progression of the spiritual journey. Newness, vitality and excitement still characterized the pursuit of private and public religion. The community was at peace, largely unaware of several developments which would soon threaten its tranquility.

NOTES

1 P.M. Friesen, *The Mennonite Brotherhood in Russia, 1789-1910* (Halbstadt, 1911), 276. See also pp. 325-326.

2 Peter Reimer, "Russland," *Zionsbote*, VII (1891), no. 18, 2; Judith Lohrenz, "Margenau, den 4. April 1891," *Zionsbote*, VII(1891), no. 20, 3-4; Heinrich Penner, "Meine Bekehrung," *Zionsbote*, X(1894), no. 38, 3.

3 "eine Gesellschaft, die meinem Fleisch sehr ansprach," Thomas Koop, "Meine Erfahrung," *Zionsbote*, VII (1891), no. 47, 1. Another spoke of the fact that he withdrew from "der weltlichen Gesellschaft," "Meine Erfahrung," *Zionsbote*, X(1894), no. 31, 2-3.

4 J. Epp, "Aus meinem Leben," *Zionsbote*, VII (1891), no. 27, 2-3; also *Zionsbote*, VII (1891), no. 23, 2.

5 Abraham Peters, "Meine Bekehrung, *Zionsbote*, VII (1891), no. 32, 1.

6 "Meine Erfahrung," *Zionsbote*, VII (1891), no. 49, 1.

7 Peter Goerzen, "Russland," *Zionsbote*, VII (1891), no. 26, 2; Johann Huebert, "Die Bekehrung eines Bruders," *Zionsbote*, X (1894), no. 20, 2; Peter Perk, "Etwas aus meinem Leben," *Zionsbote*, X (1894), no. 23, 2; Elisabeth Friesen, "Wie mich der Herr bekehrte," *Zionsbote*, X (1894), no. 29, 2-3.

8 B.B. Janz Papers (Center for Mennonite Brethren Studies in Canada, Winnipeg, Manitoba), Memoirs, "Meine Heimkehr," 8-9.

9 Henry E. Reimer, *Being Born Again by the Word of God* (n.p., n.d.), 5-6.

10 Herman Neufeld Journals (Center for Mennonite Brethren Studies in Canada, Winnipeg, Manitoba), "Lebensgeschichte," 117 ff.

11 "Ich fing an zu beten um Vergebung meiner Suenden. Ich blieb in diesem Zustand ungefaehr einen Monat, ich konnte aber nicht durchkommen." F.J. Becker, "Wie der Herr mich gesucht und gefunden hat," *Zionsbote*, X (1894) no. 32, 3. Also *Zionsbote*, X (1894), no. 33, 3-4.

12 Anna Boschman, "Wie der Herr mich gesucht und gefunden," *Zionsbote*, X (1894), no. 21, 3; K. Boschman, "Wie mich der Herr aus der Finsternis zu seinem wunderbaren Lichte gebracht hat," *Zionsbote*, X (1894), no. 21, 2-3.

13 "So lebte ich froh und konnte auch die Biblestunde fuehren und ueberlaut beten und danken." Peter Friesen, "Meine Bekehrung," *Zionsbote*, X (1894), no. 19, 2-3; Heinrich Penner, "Meine Bekehrung," *Zionsbote*, X (1894), no. 38, 3.

14 Herman Neufeld Journals, II (1904).

15 Wilhelm Loewen, "Alexanderkrone, 20 Feb. 1891," *Zionsbote*, VII (1891), no. 16, 3. J. Fast, "Reisekizzen," *Zionsbote*, VII (1891), no. 17, 1; Heinrich Friesen, Reisebericht aus Russland," *Zionsbote*, VII (1891), no.A22, 2-3.

16 Klaas Enns, "Sparrau, 1 Febr. 1894," *Zionsbote*, (1894), no. 12, 2.

17 "Margenau," *Zionsbote*, X (1894), no. 15, Beilage.

18 David Duerksen, "Reisebericht," *Zionsbote*, X (1894), No. 49, 3.
19 A number of these reports can be found in the *Zionsbote*, which published them on a regular basis. See for example Hermann Neufeld, "Russland, Nikolaijewka, im Maerz, 1895," *Zionsbote*, xl (1895), no. 17, 2; Heinrich Friesen, "Reisebericht," *Zionsbote*, Xl (1895), no. 18, 2.
20 Wilhelm Loewen, Reisebericht," *Zionsbote*, VI (1890), no. 16, 1.
21 David Duerksen, "Reisebericht," *Zionsbote*, X (1894), no. 49, 3.
22 Hermann Neufeld Journals (Centre for MB Studies, Winnipeg, Manitoba), "Rechnung von der Missionreisen 1888-1919,"
23 *Ibid.*
24 Neufeld Journals, "Unsere Lebensgeschichte" I, 348-350.
25 *Ibid.*, II, 488-490.
26 Hermann Neufeld Journals, I. Band, 199-200.
27 *Ibid.*, 208. In January, 1889 Kargel visited Friedensfeld and conducted a month long "Missionschule" which was attended by 16 Brethren. Jakob Janz "Jahresbericht von der Gemeinde Friedensfeld 1889," *Zionsbote*, Vol. 6 (1890), no. 10, 1-2.
28 For a condensed autobiography in English see Abram H. Neufeld (translator and editor), *Herman and Katharina: Their Story* (Winnipeg, The Christian Press, 1984).

CHAPTER VI
NEW HORIZONS AND OLD VALUES

The Russian Mennonite world expanded with unprecedented rapidity as the nineteenth century drew to a close. The growth of the milling and agricultural machinery industry forced some urbanization. Stable grain prices not only brought prosperity to older established farms, but ensured the survival of most new settlements as well. There was also an expansion of the Mennonite mind. This was not only due to influx of educational and religious literature from Germany but related to the Mennonite young men who studied in German and Russian institutions of higher learning. These developments coincided with government demands for state service and closer Russian cultural identification. The Mennonites responded by resorting to an institutionalism unparalleled in their history. They erected a vast, privately supported educational complex beginning at the elementary school level and culminating in a broad array of welfare, medical and advanced learning institutions. An orphanage, a school for mutes, a deaconess home, hospitals—all demanded a broad-based community involvement. Isolation and withdrawal from the common task was out of the question.

Their very origins had forced a special kind of openness upon the Brethren. The radicals among them rejected the old framework of piety. When the moderates regained control, the movement stood alone and isolated. If it was to survive, outside help was essential. This quest was not without its inconsistencies. In language, custom and economics the Brethren still belonged to the older Mennonite peoplehood. In their search for vital religion, however, they rejected virtually all aspects of their past. A successful pilgrimage amid such tensions meant accommodating compatible religious traditions wherever possible.

Wuest's legacy, while crucial in fomenting spiritual renewal, ultimately did not supply adequate sustenance for long-term discipleship. The Mennonites were never completely cut off from other Christian groups during their Russian sojourn. Diverse religious influences periodically penetrated their communities at least two decades prior to 1860. The Quakers, William Allen and Stephen Grellet, travelled through the Mennonite settlements and preached to large gatherings as early as 1819.[1] Almost simultaneously the Russian Bible Society, founded in 1812 and patterned after the British and Foreign Bible Society, began to distribute Testaments and Bibles in the Molotschna settlement. Shortly after Tobias Voth began teaching at the Ohrloff school a late candidate for the position, Daniel Schlatter from Basel, arrived on the scene. Undeterred, he began to work among the Nogai of the region and frequently interacted with elder Bernhard Fast and others. David Epp of Chortitza met the British Bible Society representative John Melville in 1842 and accepted six chests of Bibles and New Testaments for distribution.[2] Another Quaker, John Yeardley, was in contact with the Russian Mennonites in 1853.[3] Then, too, printed sermons and devotional literature began to penetrate their ethnocentric world during the 1840s and 1850s.

In a sense the Brethren-Baptist flirtation marked a continuation of the earlier openness. There were special mitigating circumstances during the 1860s. A wilful, lonely orphan needed a big brother. Timing was of the essence if the association was to be successful. In the main it was the Baptists who provided a model for a movement which found itself in an organizational and theological vacuum. Brethren radicalism needed something new and stable. Baptist church polity, preaching and theology were not that different from the dissident's aspirations. Here was a pattern into which they could fit much of their new life experience. The Baptist, Johann Oncken, for example, provided a new line of religious authority by ordaining Abraham Unger as elder in 1868.[4] Likewise, Baptists like Carl Benzier and August Liebig imposed record keeping and correct procedure upon the early, rather chaotic business meetings. Thanks to Liebig's year long residence in Andreasfeld (1871-72) the Brethren also learned about Sunday School and introduced a time of public prayer during the worship service.[5] He not only ended factionalism, but also respected their traditions, since he "left the distinctly Mennonite confession of the Brethren untouched."[6] In 1872-73 the cooperation went even further: two Baptists, Eduard Leppke

56

and Wilhelm Schutz, were appointed to the Brethren itinerant ministry.[7]

Another scenario involved the brothers Gerhard and Johann Wieler. Extremely gifted yet very different in temperament, the two played diverse roles in the early history of the Brethren. Gerhard, inclined to the ecstatic and emotional, became a leading advocate of the exuberance movement. Johann, restrained and reflective, steadily opposed the excesses of his older brother and at one point was excommunicated by him. Together the brothers nevertheless made substantial contributions in two areas. Fluent in Russian, both functioned as civil rights advocates for the hard-pressed, fledgling movement. Both were also deeply committed to evangelism and were partially responsible for the birth of the German and Russian Baptist movement in the southern Ukraine. Johann not only attended the first Convention of the Russian Baptists held in Novo-Vasilevka in 1884 but was elected as its president. Its agenda manifested Brethren overtones: the election of itinerant ministers for evangelism; the question of open communion; the issue of footwashing.[8]

The Baptist connection had its problems from the very outset. The first Brethren Confession of Faith drafted in 1873 carefully specified that the two groups were distinct from one another, yet the document itself borrowed heavily from Baptist sources. It seemed the Baptist liaison compromised the Brethren search for identity from the start. When the secessionists tried to clarify their relationship with the Baptists at their 1876 conference the item had to be postponed because it was too contentious. On one occasion before the government recognition of the Baptists in 1879, Brethren elders and ministers faced the unenviable task of trying to convince a czarist official that they were different from both the Old Church and the Baptists.[9]

Brethren-Baptist contacts were sustained by visiting speakers and the flow of Baptist theological and devotional materials during the 1880s and 1890s. Baptists frequently spoke at mission and thanksgiving festivals or served as key resource persons at Bible courses.[10] Problems continued to plague their love affair. Russian authorities frequently confused the Brethren with the Baptists and appropriate petitions clarifying the relationship were periodically drawn up. Sometimes this resulted from the ongoing fraternization, on other occasions hostile complaints by isolated members of the Old Church launched official investigations.

Towards the end of the nineteenth century there was

another area of Brethren contact. It involved their liaison with the Blankenburg *Allianz* Conference, the European counterpart to the English Darbyites or Plymouth Brethren. The Conference, founded in 1885, sponsored annual sessions in Germany which attracted international participation. Several personalities associated with the conference were to have a profound effect upon the Mennonite Brethren in Russia. These included F.W. Baedeker, Ernst F. Stroeter, F.B. Meyers, Otto Stockmayer and General von Viehbahn. Their influence was spread via one- or two-week Bible conferences in various Mennonite communities or through special lectures often sponsored by the estate owner David Dick at Apanlee.[11] The impact of their writings was possibly even more decisive. Two periodicals, *Botschafter des Heils in Christo* (Messenger of Salvation in Christ) and professor Stroeter's *Das Prophetische Wort* (The Prophetic Word), provided both Brethren and Old Church ministers with sermon material. On a more popular level their devotional calendar *Botschafter des Friedens* (Messenger of Peace) and the *Elberfelder* Bible translation circulated rather widely.

What effect did the Blankenburg Conference have on the Brethren? In some ways it marked the final stage of foreign influence on the development of Brethren piety. From the very inception of the movement pietistic and Baptist literature had been disseminated by Mennonite booksellers and through the mail. Since it was mainly devotional in character it enhanced the Brethren inclination towards the inner life. Decades of casual Baptist contact did not threaten the Brethren understanding of what it meant to be the people of God on the Russian steppes. Similarly Blankenburg theology with its concern for holy living, the inner life and the communion of the saints was generally affirming for the Brethren. There were other views which, while commendable, possibly generated some discomfort among the Brethren. Blankenburg emphasized interdenominational fellowship by arguing that external forms and denominational creedalism mattered little. There were only two ordinances uniting all the true followers of Jesus: baptism and the Lord's Supper. Though they practiced immersion baptism, Blankenburg advocates did not make the baptismal mode a condition of membership. Similarly its communion celebrations were open to all true believers. The Blankenburg *Allianz* Conference, deeply rooted in its culture, readily identified with German nationalism and even militarism. It was a trifle ironic that Blankenburg's intensification of Mennonite piety, especially among the

58

Brethren, also diluted the commitment to nonresistence. In later years some leaders attributed the widespread support of the *Selbstschutz* during the anarchy of 1918-19 directly to this foreign theological influence.

The nature of *Allianz* influence upon the Brethren was partially illustrated by the observations of one, Jakob Huebert. In 1909 he returned to visit his co-religionists in South Russia after a sixteen year absence. He was overwhelmed by the prevailing spiritual vitality. There were, in his estimation, "only a few unconverted among the ministers."[12] He was impressed by the many Bible conferences *(Bibelbesprechungen)* which in their emphasis were practical, informative and promoted fellowship. "Much is expected and given in the preaching of the Word, even though many ministers are lay brothers... if there is anywhere where great things have been done for God's kingdom by the laity it is among the Mennonites of South Russia."[13] Huebert pointed to the intense home and foreign mission activity, the promotion of schools, the erection of broad-ranging benevolent institutions. Such goodness stemmed from a common will and united striving. "If it should ever come to the point where there is an attempt to eliminate the lay ministry and lay participation, then God will take his blessing from our people."[14] Especially noteworthy was the closer cooperation between the two churches.[15] There was a "striving towards *Allianz* (togetherness)" promoted by "the foreign religious workers which came to Russia from time to time."[16]

Huebert's observations clearly reflected some aspects of the Blankenburg impact upon the Brethren. By stressing the inner life and focusing on essentials, the movement encouraged them to cross denominational lines. Together with members in the Old Church they focused on missions, welfare, benevolence and the promotion of literacy. Interest in foreign missions intensified while here and there courageous individuals among the laity began to preach to neighboring Russians. Likewise, the growth of Mennonite social awareness was usually spearheaded by compassionate laymen. Their concern for the deprived, the aged, the sick, the parentless and the mentally handicapped induced them to devote their talents and money to institutional development. As the various institutions emerged, others in the constituency caught their vision. There was another dimension in the evolving social conscience of the early twentieth century: the constituency began to respond to regions afflicted by natural disasters, usually by providing famine relief.

The expanded religious awareness nurtured by Bible courses and conferences spawned another kind of radical vision—evangelism among the Russians. This had always been something of a problem for both the Brethren and the Old Church. The terms under which they settled in Russia only guaranteed religious freedom to the Mennonites but said little about the right to proselytize.[17] The law prohibiting evangelism among members of the Russian Orthodox Church was contained in one of several manifestoes (1863) issued by Catherine II in her efforts to attract foreign colonists to Russia.[18] In general the decree was rather rigorously observed even though most Mennonite settlements adjoined orthodox populations. Furthermore, few Mennonites felt at home in the Russian language or culture until almost the end of the nineteenth century.

The early twentieth century interest in evangelism among the Russians was rooted in several factors. The reactionary policies of Alexander III (1881-1894) and his chief advisor, Constantine Pobedonostsev were somewhat modified by the provisions contained in the October Manifesto of 1905. Because it granted freedom of conscience, most Mennonites, though scarcely aware of the magnitude of the tensions engulfing Russia, sensed a new freedom of movement. Then, too, periodic revivals in various settlements, some spontaneous others inspired by itinerant ministers, generated a new consciousness of mission. For a number of the later missionaries their own spectacular conversions were often accompanied by an overwhelming sense of calling to evangelize the Russians. Brethren and Old Church Mennonites, long accustomed to sending Gospel emissaries to Athens and Rome, now became aware that just beyond Jerusalem lay Judea and Samaria. In the end, missions to which they were so committed, generated problems for the Brethren.

Recounting his early religious pilgrimage, the Old Church adherent Peter Riediger wrote:

> When I experienced a personal conversion in the year 1900 the Lord in his great mercy also gave me a love for the Russians. Since I not only had daily contact with our workers but with many others I occasionally read the Scriptures to them and pointed them to the way of salvation. That was not enough for the Lord. He wanted all the workers in our village to hear the good tidings and He showed me—the way. During the winter of 1905-1906 we held Russian services in our home. About 50 Russians, men

and women, came regularly. I always got brother Adolf Reimer, who was a teacher in Tiege, to preach. Brother Adolf Reimer was a member of the Mennonite Brethren church and I still belonged to the Old Church, but we were of one mind. The Lord blessed his word and a number received it and gave themselves to the Lord.[19]

Ironically, opposition to their efforts came from two sources: the Mennonite and Russian Orthodox clergy.[20]

Peter Riediger's somewhat rambling account lists the evangelists known to him personally: the Old Church member Fedrau active in the Crimea; a Cornelius Janz who preached in the Orenburg-Samara region; a Jacob Wiens living in the city of Samara. Riediger's memoir also mentions H.P. Sukkau in Neu-Samara, the Bernhard Klassens in Siberia and a Johann Peters and his associates who went to live among the Yakuts of eastern Siberia. Adolf A. Reimer (1891-1921) was something of a central figure in the work among the Russians. He resigned his teaching post in the Molotschna in order to take up an itinerant ministry among the Russians. His reports in the *Friedensstimme* find him preaching in cities like St. Petersburg and Kharkov, in factories, on the estates of the Russian nobility, in Russian villages, among convicts or to young, struggling Russian congregations.[21] He remained active during the civil war preaching to both Red and White army troops, finally succumbing to typhus after an extended ministry in the Kiev area.

Riediger concludes his account with the words: "I knew all these people."[22] A few pages earlier he observed: "Aside from these jottings only eternity will reveal how many of our Mennonites carried on missions among the Russians. I believe [my memoir] reflects only a small part of what was actually done."[23]

The Riediger document reveals some surprising facts about the pattern of Russian evangelism. It was extremely individualistic. Concerned men and women simply took action. Riediger invited Russian workers into his home and requested Adolf Reimer to preach. H.P. Sukkau moved to a Russian town in order to learn Russian and worked as a carpenter to support his family. Johann Peters and his friends journeyed into the high arctic, adopted the Yakut life style and earned their livelihood by fishing with them. Jacob Wiens lived in the city of Samara as a Bible salesman. On a visit to the Brethren church at Lugovsk he induced the congregation to hold evangelistic services in a large neighboring Russian village. Their activities were as varied as the individuals involved. Some simply testified to their workers or the Russians they encountered, others held house meetings, and those who were capable, travelled and preached.

Evangelism among the Russians also reflected a sense of the spontaneous. A Russian couple invited a trembling, unsure Peter Riediger to their village. He hardly spoke a word before a widespread revival erupted.[24] Adolf Reimer preached wherever and whenever the opportunity presented itself. Riediger reports that H.P. Sukkau "preached God's Word in all the nearby Russian villages. Everywhere lost sinners accepted the Word and gave themselves to the Lord."[25] Citing Jacob Wiens of the city of Samara, Riediger writes:

> Look at brother H.P. Sukkau's influence! There is hardly a village where he has not been where there is not a smaller or a larger church. Yet for the educated [people] he is not the right man.[26]

Riediger also referred to the clothes worn by men like Sukkau and Peters—"boots and plain [loose] clothing"[27]—the garb of the Russian peasant.

The larger constituency was not involved in Russian evangelism. Riediger is explicit.

> Both conferences the Mennonite and the Mennonite Brethren, remained silent. A minority even protested against those who carried on mission [work] among the Russians. Some feared the police, others wanted to live in peace and quiet.[28]

The support for these intinerant evangelists usually came from a few missionary-minded local churches or individuals.

> Brother H.P. Sukkau was not appointed or supported by any church. Faithful children of God sustained him with prayer and with offerings for his family.[29]

Most lived under very marginal circumstances. Perhaps their common zeal was best characterized by Riediger's refreshing observation that

> Whenever there were Mennonites—in the south, in the east, in the north—there were those who had no peace or quiet in their heart when they saw the ignorant and the misled. The love of Jesus Christ drove them...to speak to this people.[30]

The lack of constituency support usually meant that the individual evangelists connected with those who shared their vision. An H.P. Sukkau first began to preach in Russian in a small Baptist Church and later carried out some of his ministry under Baptist auspices. Riediger prosaically concludes his report of evangelism in the Poltava region with the sentence: "Thus Russian Baptist churches were founded there."[31] Jacob Wiens worked with a Molokan and a Russian officer in the city of Samara and founded an evangelical church there. A Cornelius Janzen came to the same city to evangelize. He contacted typhus and after a brief illness died, "surrounded by dear, sympathetic Russian brothers and sisters."[32] After Peter Riediger's ministry brought revival to a Russian village, over 60 "newly converted souls were examined, baptized and accepted into the church at Novo Petrofka."[33] It was a Baptist congregation.

During the 1860s adverse pressures had forced the Brethren to look for new friends. The Baptists with their established constituency and similar theology offered interim security. Ongoing contacts throughout the later nineteenth century allowed both groups to clarify their association. The relationship did not threaten the Brethren for by then they had forged a separate peoplehood within Russian Mennonitism. The Blankenburg relationship was more complex. As in the case of the Baptists there were the familiar beliefs, the German cultural roots and the substantial spiritual nurture. Blankenburg's insistence on fellowship and unity amidst denominational distinctions nevertheless threatened Brethren identity. The majority were not ready to become something else. This tension coincided with another kind of intellectual-spiritual expansiveness. By the early twentieth century the Brethren, whether living in frontier villages or in the older established settlements, participated fully in the changing Mennonite world. Many of their young men and women, like those of the Old Church, completed high school as well as teachers or nurses training. Some went on to German or Russian universities to study theology, law or medicine. Added to this were the voices of dedicated and sincere persons who were preaching the Gospel to Russians. These demanded that the Brethren should begin to feel at home among the Russians. There was uneasiness in the Brethren soul. Too much was being asked too soon. Discontinuity threatened continuity. Amidst all the expanding awareness there remained significant remnants of an earlier, essentially rural piety which was reluctant to enlarge its horizons. Two forces worked at cross purposes. On the one hand there was something of the open existential dynamic of the movement's founding years which, nurtured by foreign influences, continued to grow. On the other, there were elements of the conservative, the rigid and isolationistic. A segment of the one-time radicals was becoming reactionary. Unwittingly and almost simultaneously they were becoming both the liberal and conservative.

NOTES

1 Richenda C. Scott, *Quakers in Russia* (London, 1964), 113ff.
2 David Epp Diary (Mennonite Heritage Center, Winnipeg, Man.) July 19, 1842. See also James Urry, "John Melville and the Mennonites: A British Evangelist in South Russia, 1837-c.1875," *Mennonite Quarterly Review*, LIV, (1980), no. 4, 305-322.
3 Charles Tylor (ed.), *Memoir of John Yeardley* (London, 1859), 19, 400, 402-414; *Allen, William, Life and Correspondence* (London, 1846), II, 19-93.
4 P.M. Friesen *Alt-Evangelische Mennonitische Bruederschaft in Russland* (Halbstadt, Taurien, 1911), 382-384.
5 *Ibid.*
6 *Ibid.*, 386.
7 *Ibid.*, 395.
8 *Ibid.*, 367-68; 411; 414-416; 430-35; 601-601; Alexander Karov, The Russian Evangelical Baptist Movement (manuscript in possession of the Southern Baptist Historical Commission), 110-111.
9 Friesen, 397-399.
10 Hermann Neufeld recorded the ministry of two Baptists at the annual Brethren conference in 1907. One of them was the German Baptist mission inspector Karl Maschner from Berlin. Hermann Neufeld Journals (Center for Mennonite Brethren Studies in Canada, Winnipeg, Manitoba), II (1904), 199-201.
11 G. Harder, "Reisebericht," *Friedensstimme*, IV (1906), no. 23, 239; G. Unruh, "Der Bibelkursus in Waldheim," VII (1909), no. 50, 2-3; M. Huebert, "Zwei Segenstage in Lichtfelde," *Friedensstimme* VII (1909), no.A38, 3-4.
12 J. Huebert, "Meine Eindruecke von dem Leben unserer Mennoniten in Suedrussland," *Friedensstimme*, VII (1909), no. 45, 3.
13 *Ibid.*
14 *Ibid.*
15 *Ibid.*
16 *Ibid.*
17 David G. Rempel, "The Mennonite Commonwealth in Russia. A Sketch of its Founding and Endurance, 1789-1919," *Mennonite Quarterly Review*, XVLII, no. 4 (October, 1973), 283-286.
18 *Ibid.*, 269.
19 B.B. Janz Papers (Center for Mennonite Brethren Studies, Winnipeg, Manitoba), Peter Riediger, "Mission der Mennoniten in Russland unter den Russen." 4-5.

[20] *Ibid.*, 4-5.
[21] Adolf Reimer, "Bilder aus der Arbeit unter den Russen," *Friedensstimme*, V (1907), no. 11, 128-129; Adolf Reimer, "Reiseerfahrungen," *Friedensstimme*, VII (1909), no. 44, 4.
[22] Riediger, 30.
[23] *Ibid.*, 27.
[24] *Ibid.*, 24ff.
[25] *Ibid.*, 20.
[26] *Ibid.*, 18.
[27] *Ibid.*, 30.
[28] *Ibid.*, 2-3.
[29] *Ibid.*, 18.
[30] *Ibid.*, 3.
[31] *Ibid.*, 8.
[32] *Ibid.*, 8-9.
[33] *Ibid.*, 26.

CHAPTER VII
CRISIS

Following his election to the itinerant ministry in 1888, Hermann Neufeld's prosaic journal entries almost camouflage the excitement of ongoing conversions and baptisms. It was simply the way things should be: the preaching of the Gospel meant new life for sinners and edification for the saints. Periodic revivals are almost taken for granted. He complains to his journal only when there are few conversions and baptisms.

The tone of his entries changes noticeably as the twentieth century approaches. Yearly preaching journeys take him far from home for long periods of time. He speaks less of conversion and church growth. Neufeld was frustrated by two very different situations. The first involved his partnership in a milling venture. His colleagues were obstinate and uncooperative. The second issue related to the question of communion.Neufeld held to the Brethren tradition that only those baptized by immersion took part in the service. Here was a man, himself the product of Brethren evangelism, preoccupied with the mode of baptism and communion exclusiveness. In 1897 elder David Schellenberg requested him to visit the Blankenburg *Allianz* Conference in Germany. Though he enjoyed the proceedings, he could not bring himself to participate in the closing communion service.

Was Neufeld's response indicative of a larger ongoing crisis? What was happening to the evangelizing, nurturing Brethren of earlier decades? On the surface little seemed to change. The Brethren fully participated in the widespread economic expansion characterized by industrialization and agricultural mechanization. Their religious quest seemed equally energetic. The earlier Bible courses became Bible Conferences featuring articulate, highly trained preachers and lecturers from Germany.

67

The theology of these and other visitors was generally affirming. How could all these expanding experiences suddenly allow an all-consuming focus on the narrow, confining issue of open or closed communion?

For decades a type of restricted communion had been practiced in Brethren circles. In part their very secession was instigated as a protest against the undiscerning communion practiced in the Old Church. From the beginning it was simply understood that only the baptized adherents of the new movement participated in the celebration. Since immersion baptism became an important symbol differentiating the Brethren from the Old Church, the ordinance mode easily became equated with true faith and genuine spirituality. Baptists, with their explicit views on conversion and immersion baptism, constituted no threat and were readily admitted to Brethren communion services and even church membership. When revival penetrated segments of the Old Church at the turn of the century and brought Christian social action on many fronts, the communion question reached a crisis point.

In his compilation of documents and personal reminiscences A.H. Unruh includes an 1899 incident penned by Jakob Thiessen.[1] The teacher Penner in Steinbach (Molotschna) expressed a desire for baptism during a visit of the Brethren leader Jakob Reimer. Arrangements were hastily made. A visitor requested that all true believers be allowed to attend the examination of the candidate and participate in the communion after baptism. Jakob Reimer, inclined towards open communion thanks to his involvement with the Blankenburg Conference, assented. As it turned out only two Old Church members participated. Severe objections to Reimer's liberality not only erupted at the next congregational meeting but became a sequential agenda item at future Brethren conferences.

When he attended the annual conference in 1900, Hermann Neufeld noted that "the discussions concerning open communion with unrebaptized believers in which I participated were not pleasant."[2] At the 1903 conference in Waldheim, Molotschna, the discussions were calmer, "yet many hearts did not remain calm."[3] When a vote was called for which, in Neufeld's judgement, "was not according to the will of God,"[4] 13 delegates supported open communion while 59 were opposed.[5] Ten abstained from the vote.

Pressure against the liberal minority increased at the 1904 conference. Jakob Reimer and Jakob Kroeker were not reappointed to the itinerant ministry.[6] In part the differences were regional. Einlage in Chortitza favored closed communion while the large Rueckenau church, led by Jakob Reimer, not only inclined towards open communion but practiced it. Following Reimer's dismissal as a conference worker, pressure against him mounted. In Reimer's Rueckenau congregation some interpreted this and later conference resolutions as a request for his dismissal. Others saw it as pressure designed to force Reimer to join the Evangelical Mennonite Brotherhood (*Allianz*) in Lichtfelde, with whom he had close connections.[8]

Open communion remained a contentious issue for some years. Conference discussions involving the conservative majority and a vocal, influential minority usually ended in a stalemate. Resolutions advocating continued toleration, goodwill and brotherhood followed. The question apparently came to a head at a local meeting in Schoental in the Crimea. In Hermann Neufeld's words:

> On the third festive day [of Easter] we held a large and blessed brotherhood meeting at which among other things, we decided that like the Einlage church, we would have no further fellowship with the Rueckenau church or similiar minded ones unless they conformed to the Brethren confession of faith in matters relating to communion and baptism.[10]

There was no mention of open communion at the 1910 annual conference. Again Neufeld had an explanation. Since an official observer from St. Petersburg was present "the question of the *Allianz* could not be discussed openly. There were serious discussions and even harsh confrontations in the [executive] council."[11] External pressures finally helped to bring an end to the conflict. As early as 1908 St. Petersburg lawgivers announced their intentions of drafting new regulations for the various religious minorities in Russia. In part the retention of historic Mennonite privileges now depended on a common front. Then, too, the outbreak of World War I enhanced anti-German sentiments. Intense discussions and consultations finally produced an "evangelical Mennonite Confession" of faith. It included all three groups, the Old Church, the Brethren and the Allianz. Whether the "inner" journey of the Brethren had actually graduated towards broader tolerance remained an open question.

At the height of the open communion controversy the Rueckenau church best illustrated the Brethren dilemma. It sheltered both Jakob Reimer, popular evangelist and open communion practitioner, and elder David Schellenberg, an advocate of closed communion. The latter supported Reimer's dismissal from the itinerant ministry when the matter came before the Rueckenau congregation. A few years later (1909) Schellenberg himself was deposed as elder.[13] Some spoke of bookkeeping irregularities in the various funds entrusted to the elder; others pointed to irregularities associated with his second marriage. The issues underlying the attack on the unfortunate elder were probably broader. Brethren narrowness and exclusiveness experienced increasing theological discomfort as the surrounding religious world expanded. As apprehensions intensified a reactionary conference deposed an itinerant minister while a liberal congregation moved against an orthodox elder.

As he neared the end of his monumental study in 1910, P.M. Friesen pondered why a people given to missions and evangelism for decades had become tardy in their own spiritual growth. Was the beauty of late nineteenth-century piety fading? The prevailing tempo of Christian activity hardly supported such a conclusion. Itinerant ministers still reported their evangelistic and deeper life services. Revivals and baptisms were still the order of the day. The response to the widespread Bible courses and conferences was generally enthusiastic. Home and foreign missions found strong support. Special conferences and workshops infused new vigor into the Sunday School movement. There was Brethren affirmation of welfare and benevolence projects. Sunday morning choirs made their appearance during the 1890s and before long choral festivals became a regular feature of Brethren congregational life. According to Hermann Neufeld the 1894 Rueckenau *Saengerfest* attracted 2,000 listeners and featured 300 singers from eleven choirs. New songs and new tempos were not foreign to such a setting, yet were not considered too innovative. This continued capacity for openness and accommodation was perhaps illustrated by the visit of Franz Wiens, an American missionary to China, who had come to solicit support among the Mennonites in South Russia. His preaching and singing "made a deep impression" on his listeners. At the close of his dramatic sermons he asked those wishing to decide for Christ to stand up or raise their hands. The results were spectacular. Within one week 120 persons were converted while some 60 testified in a single meeting. Neufeld reported that although the brethren did not "understand his style," they made no request for a less rigorous style of evangelism.[14]

How could all this preaching, singing and learning slow

down spiritual growth and incline the Brethren soul to the narrow and the insular? Was there some impure residue which became a slow-growing cancer and eventually crippled a vibrant organism? Had the delicate tension between inner experience and discipleship, successfully maintained since 1865, shifted in favor of feeling rather than following? Were the Brethren succumbing to the classic dangers confronting pietism whereby the celebration of the inner life became such a consuming passion that it blocked the spontaneous expression of goodness in everyday life? Had discipleship, deprived of nourishment, withered and degenerated into a separatistic loveless legalism? Had inner experience, unable to sustain feeling and emotion indefinitely, resorted to cliches and comforting words in order to mistakenly create the ongoing illusion of vitality?

Brethren reality was probably never that categorical. One realm never excluded the other. Yet if Friesen was right in his observations there were elements of the crippling and debilitating. How amid all the constraining and balancing forces could the shift towards the experiential occur? Some elements in the style of Brethren piety may have contributed. Brethren services were much given to short sermons, testifying and singing. In the early 1860s joy expressed itself through flutes, triangles, tambourines and drums. Both the content and tempo of the songs represented a radical departure from the typical old church setting with its *Vorsaenger* (song leader) and his often capricious treatment of traditional melodies.

Heinrich Franz attempted to bring order and harmony to Mennonite hymn singing with his compilation of a *Choralbuch* begun in 1837 and finally published in a four-part edition in 1860. Notated in ciphers (*Ziffern*) it was used first in village schools and only gradually adopted in the churches. A new hymnal did not always mean new singing. Opposition to *Zifferngesang* (cipher singing) was widespread. The large Chortitza church only adopted it in 1865. According to Jacob Epp's diary there were those who stormed out of the church whenever the new melodies were sung, or boycotted services for months on end.[15] How could a society which had difficulty accepting Franz's hymnal ever hope to understand the musical antics of the early Brethren? In their radicalism they not only rejected Franz's hymnal but borrowed three foreign ones—*Glaubensstimme, Frohe Botschaft* and *Heimatklaenge*. Then, utilizing the infinite capacity of the German language for combination, fused these into one—the *Dreiband*.

After examining the 1,079 hymns in the *Dreiband* collection one scholar concluded that only two were of "Anabaptist derivation."[16] In his estimation the majority of the other songs were "subjective and experiential."[17] These new songs with their emphasis on sin, atonement and the new life experience easily integrated into the informal Brethren meetings with their alternating testimonies, prayers, Scripture readings and brief sermons. They enhanced the emotional, inward-looking content of such gatherings. Here were words and melodies which became important components of an ongoing lay theology. This type of religious practice not only spoke of the experiential but regularly recreated it as well.

Jakob Reimer, commenting on monthly Saturday meetings conducted by the early Brethren, spoke of "*selige Nachmittagsstunden* (blessed afternoon hours), during which our hearts were filled with Jesus' love."[18] Songs were an integral part of such celebration. Can such a holy and sacred setting endure a moment of cynicism? Was it possible that the new songs with their vivid imagery and stirring melodies actually constituted an accumulative danger? Could they not create a religious sentiment so strongly emotional in character that it circumscribed the study and preaching of the Word? Did the song writer subtly generate an emotionally oriented theology which resisted any knowledge of divine truth not capable of eliciting familiar feelings? If so, the resulting interdependency of faith and feeling forced a narrow tradition upon the Brethren.

The cycle of private and public assemblies evoked familiar pious emotions which in turn became the measure of spiritual progress. The piety which nourished and delighted the soul was often restricted to a recounting of the penitential agony and the salvation process. Practiced for decades it stultified Christian maturation. It inconspicuously reinforced the inclination towards the narrow and restrictive even in a setting saturated with special conferences, periodic festivals, weekly worship services and frequent Bible studies.

Though they would not have known what the term meant the post-1865 Brethren practiced an existential theology. They tried to apply the Gospel to the varying circumstances of life. The shift back to the experiential was subtle. There was no shouting, jumping or drumbeating—only the quiet, dignified cultivation of heartfelt emotion. How could one suspect feelings of well-being? Yet how readily such sensitivities promoted the status quo, since they were self-authenticating. They were also self-vindicating, since they easily silenced criticism: it was not proper to question sacred emotion. Unfortunately, the restricted cycle of emotional piety circumscribed the pursuit of discipleship. Discipleship, less interested in the issues of the everyday and less engaging of the world at large, increasingly reverted to a fixed pattern of goodness generally regarded as normative to faith. As discipleship became a measurable performance it tried to anticipate every possible behavioral deviation whether it pertained to hair and dress styles or the the kind of vocabulary used in religious conversation. Piousness (*Froemmigkeit*) emerged in stark contrast to worldliness (*Weltlichkeit*).

The shift in favor of the experiential did not produce a dramatic decline in religious vitality. The quality of Brethren peoplehood remained largely unchanged but its ability to appeal to a broader spectrum of Mennonite society was significantly reduced. In a sense the Evangelical Mennonite Brotherhood stepped into the gap left by the Brethren. Here was the same commitment to new life, holy living and evangelism. Ironically, the Brethren suffered significant losses to a movement with which they were in complete theological agreement. There was really only one difference: the *Allianz* invited all believers to communion regardless of baptismal mode.

There were other kinds of losses. The experiential bias, seeking to sustain the status quo, led to a creedalized theology. Concepts traditionally associated with salvation—*Busse* (repentance) and *Bekehrung* (conversion) became narrowly prescribed pathways. The examination of baptismal candidates *(Aussprache)* demanded a uniformity of response reminiscent of the catechism practices in the Old Church. Instead of rejoicing in the flexibility and expanding borders of the believer's church the experiential bias demanded a separated church, a confined peoplehood. Closely related was the desire for a discipleship associated with vigorously defined ethics. The enjoyment of the experiential bias may also have dampened Brethren social awareness. They were participants but not leaders in the quest for societal betterment among the Russian Mennonites. Religious ecstasy wanted to remain alone with Jesus. At times it forgot His mercy also extended to the aged, the orphans and the handicapped of every description.

Brethren narrowness in an expanding religious world may have been related to something other than the subtle celebration of the experiential. The Brethren, like most dissenters in their search for stability, began to regard earlier group views and practices as sacrosanct and unassailable. Leaders, unsure of their ground or simply conservative, appealed to the "faith of the fathers" or customary usage in order to defend their course of action. Some Brethren leaders of the late nineteenth century inadvertently fit such a pattern. Drawn from the congregation, self-educated or at best nurtured by a short *Bibelkursus* they emerged as ready defenders of the denominational tradition. In the context of frontier settlements where men with talent and training were especially difficult to find, insecure leaders naturally clung to practices which were known and familiar.

At the turn of the century Neufeld's journals frequently mention consultative gatherings of itinerant ministers and church leaders. The constant preoccupation with open or closed communion at these meetings suggests another closely related dynamic. The leadership core of the Brethren was readily identifiable and rather static. Their regular participation in consultations, special lectures and Bible courses solidified their ranks. Such common experience somewhat removed them from the rank and file, at least when compared with earlier decades. Most were both attracted and threatened by *Allianz*. Generally they affirmed its theology but rejected its ecumenicalism. This exposure combined with a maturing Brethren tradition possibly diffused the earlier existential theology with elements of the formal and dogmatic. The Brethren's first, self-formulated Confession of Faith in 1902 exhibited overtones of this trend. An "official" clergy needed an "official" theology. While the situation reflected denominational maturity and self-confidence it also suggested that the movement had lost something of its initial lay character.

All this did not mean that Brethren piety was repulsive or grossly inadequate. In all likelihood ministers, laymen, and even casual observers, would have given a unanimous verdict of normalcy. The experiential, though focusing mainly on itself, nevertheless operated within the borders of a secure peoplehood. Much of the old virtue was still there, but the chance for excellence was lost, at least for the moment. Claims to living faith and authentic baptism now had to be shared with the *Allianz* movement. There was even more discomfort. Brethren-style conversions were increasingly in evidence among Old Church members. New visions and new horizons were no longer Brethren prerogatives.

NOTES

[1] A.H. Unruh, *Die Geschichte der Mennoniten Bruedergemeinde 1860-1954* (Winnipeg, 1955), 229-233.

[2] Hermann Neufeld Journals (Center for Mennonite Brethren Studies in Canada), I (1904), 276-277.

[3] *Ibid.*, 316.

[4] *Ibid.*

[5] *Ibid.*, Neufeld cites 52 as being opposed. The official minutes record 59. "Bericht uber die Jahressitzung in Waldheim, vom 17-20 Mai, 1903," *Zionsbote*, Vol. 20 (1904), no. 1, 2.

[6] Neufeld Journals I (1904), 346-47.

[7] Unruh, 228.

[8] *Ibid.*, 231-232.

[9] Neufeld Journal I (1904), 485.

[10] For the minutes see "Jahressitzung der Vereinigten Christlichen Taufgesinnten Mennonitenbruedergemeinden in Russland am 14 und 15 Mai 1910 zu Tiege, Sagradowka," *Friedensstimme*, VII(1910), no. 21, 3-4; no. 22, 4-5.

[11] Neufeld Journals, I (1904), 497.

[12] Unruh, 280ff.

[13] Unruh, 233-35; B.B. Janz Papers (Center for Mennonite Brethren Studies, Winnipeg, Manitoba), File 52h.

[14] Neufeld Journals, I (1904), 525-528.

[15] Jacob Epp Diary (Mennonite Heritage Center, Winnipeg, Manitoba), March 20, 1866; April 7, 1868; April 21, 1868; April 24, 1868; April 28, 1868; February 9, 1869; December 31, 1869; February 8, 1870.

[16] Hans Kasdorf, "Pietist Roots of Early Mennonite Brethren Spirituality," *Direction*, XIII (1984), no. 3, 50.

[17] *Ibid.*

[18] P.M. Friesen, *Die Alt-Evangelische Mennonitische Bruederschaft in Russland 1789-1910* (Halbstadt, Taurien), 169.

CHAPTER VIII
LOVING THE BROTHER

Mennonites in Russia quarrelled before 1860. They argued with their leaders during settlement and with each other afterwards. There were the Flemish and the Frisians and those in between. Elders offended congregations and were deposed. Mennonite religious leaders were confronted by Mennonite civil authorities anxious for greater control of the community. There were those with land and those without—and the shouts of the quarrel reached the highest levels of Russian government. In one sense the Brethren secession of 1860 reaffirmed continuity in the history of a rather contentious people. In another it resurrected forgotten religious values and so challenged existing ideas and practices. Somehow the very fabric of the Russian Mennonite soul was more deeply involved. Other disputes were forgotten in time. This one was not. Then too the geographic setting of the quarrel was a restrictive one. The narrow confines of the mid-century village mindset easily retained the memories of angry words spoken or harsh actions taken. Some of these were factually correct, some error prone, others false. In later decades it proved difficult to re-examine these early images.

Basic to the Old Church image of the Brethren was the extreme nature of their early religious style. In the wake of the Neu-Kronsweide revival in 1853-1854 radical leaders encouraged loud hallelujahs, lively rhythms with percussion accompaniment, the sister kiss and the rejection of everything associated with the old piety. Initially they were deemed worthy of the name *Frommen* (the pious ones) but soon derisive terms like *Froehliche* (the joyous ones), *Huepfer* (jumpers) and *Springer* (springers) seemed more appropriate. Thanks to the early antics of the nonconformists the Chortitza version of a Brethren "sin catalogue" was probably compiled by 1858. The excesses of the few spoiled it for the moderate many since the prevailing rumors and exaggerations stemmed from their activities. Generally images of Brethren piety related to the sensational and unbecoming and the quietistic, contemplative elements in the movement were soon forgotten. Such a "sin catalogue," orally transmitted and enhanced by spectacular stories prevented any meaningful dialogue over the decades.

Even if it wanted to do so the old structure could hardly have exercised moderation, for the Brethren too had compiled a "sin catalogue" the details of which were largely spelled out in the secession document. They were concerned with the inability of the old system to separate the committed from the uncommitted. It administered baptism and the Lord's Supper to both groups, a practice considered unbiblical by the dissenters. The old religion also preached an inadequate gospel, especially as it pertained to the question of conversion. Such a fervent condemnation of the Old Church demanded separation. In the end baptism by immersion, though not mentioned in the secession document, not only became an indispensable symbol of new life for the individual but the final act of separation from the Old Church as well. In submitting to this ordinance the convert deliberately moved out of what he or she considered a conventional, formalized Christianity into a personalized intimate "brother-sister" setting. Family and societal crises were among the expected consequences of such a transfer. In a sense one joined the persecuted and despised.

In February, 1862, a Wilhelm Janzen of Kronsweide was severely beaten by the local mayor and imprisoned in an unheated room.[1] Here was another memory of the Old Church which the Brethren found difficult to forget. For a number of the early Brethren dissent meant imprisonment. In May, 1862, Jacob Epp reported how "their leaders Heinrich Neufeld, Abraham Unger and Johann Isaac were arrested and transported to prison."[2] A month later he reported the arrest and imprisonment of Johann Toews and Peter Nickel of Nieder Chortitz.[3] Some dissident school teachers lost their positions. There were also threats of banishment and loss of Mennonite privileges.[4] Such actions, often undertaken by elders in co-operation with the Mennonite state, were nevertheless collectively laid to the charge of the Old Church. The memories of these early persecutions tended to endure.

Extreme "official images" sustained by radical actions only

marked the beginning of the separation. Politics were also involved. The existing structure of Mennonite peoplehood tolerated little novelty, even though it was sustained by a long egalitarian tradition. Religious revisionism was simply an attack on the very fabric of Mennonitism. Many of the orthodox viewed the ideas of the Brethren as a threat to the existing religious world. When the secessionists went beyond ideological dissent and proceeded to create a new ecclesiastical structure a harsh response was inevitable.

The actual dynamics of the conflict were not that simple. The very "soul" of Russian Mennonitism was in flux. Though some actions were taken by civil authorities and others by ecclesiastical leaders, there was no unanimity of opinion as to the danger constituted by the movement. While the majority opposed the Brethren there were also those who advocated toleration. In the end the conflicts between the different levels of authority ensured Brethren survival. The crucial support of the Ohrloff Church for example, may have stemmed not only from a genuine support of Brethren religious aspirations but also from a desire to regain some of the civil authority it had lost in earlier years.

Once political co-existence became possible, religious questions tended to dominate Brethren relations with the Old Church. One such issue clearly involved the Brethren concept of conversion. The new piety was theologically sure of its salvation. As previously indicated, Brethren conversions came to reflect an amazing uniformity. As time progressed the definition of conversion became increasingly precise. Being "Brethren" meant being a believer. Many felt that while new life was possible in the Old Church its survival and nurture in that setting was rather doubtful. For those who joined the Brethren there was a strong temptation to demand that family and friends duplicate the pattern of one particular religious experience. Under such circumstances the price of a continued relationship with family and friends was a high one. Few were able to sustain it and splits within the extended family were frequent.

Meanwhile another development in the evolution of the Brethren added to the relational crisis. The scenario was a bit complicated. The early decades of the Brethren movement coincided with the establishment of new Mennonite settlements throughout European Russia. As part of the larger Mennonite community the young church was naturally involved in this dispersion process. New frontiers threatened cohesiveness. The Brethren developed a very effective strategy designed to preserve unity and even promote growth through evangelism—the itinerant ministry. Congregational growth among the Brethren was largely based on this kind of activity. Except for occasional revivals the increase was gradual and most converts came from the Old Church. Such a situation, lasting right into the twentieth century, hardly promoted goodwill between the two groups. David Epp, writing in *Der Botschafter* in 1910, observed: "The Mennonite Brethren as before, are still concerned with making proselytes among the Mennonites.[5]

The itinerant ministry created an operational piety which not only ensured stability and continuity but possibly even created a new sense of religious peoplehood. Its agenda included home visitation, Bible studies, edificatory meetings in village schools, and large assemblies at mission and thanksgiving festivals.[6] Such dedication to the cultivation of personal and public religion generated a steady reaffirmation of a distinct Brethren identity. Here were Russian Mennonites with a different religious style. That style not only included a different conversion theology and baptismal mode, but also distinct forms of Christian nurture. A common religious outlook and liturgy transcended the dispersing effect of Brethren migration to new frontiers and produced a strong sense of belonging, even in small, remote communities. In such a setting intimacy with members of the Old Church gradually became less urgent.

The Brethren flirtation with the Baptists was a contentious issue for the Old Church from the beginning. Why did the Baptist question become such a barrier to inter-Mennonite understanding, especially since many in the Old Church had also broadened the base of their spiritual quests through foreign contacts? The answer is probably not too complex. The conservative majority had its customs and traditions, its ecclesiastical leadership and liturgical patterns. The dissenting minority by rejecting the old created a vacuum which had to be filled. Baptists with their theology, preaching styles and church polity intact were readily available in the 1860s and 1870s. Here was a big brother for the wilful but lonely orphan. The price of friendship meant tolerating Baptist militarism and tobacco smoke, but with it came a group capable of sound biblical teaching and preaching, committed to the believers' church and the immersionist baptismal mode.

The Baptist connection was sustained by ongoing contacts during the 1880s and 1890s. The problems continued as well. Several Baptist related issues still fueled inter-Mennonite tensions early in the twentieth century. Brethren allowed Baptist believers to participate in their communion services on the basis of their immersion baptism, but often refused to admit believing Mennonites baptized by sprinkling. Generally Baptists were accepted as members in Brethren congregations without rebaptism while adults baptized on faith in the Old Church were rebaptized by immersion.[7] Baptist ministers were usually allowed to preach in Brethren meeting houses while Mennonite preachers were not.

The Baptist connection, a separate peoplehood, a defined conversion, village politics, mutual memories of past hurts and excesses—were the things which divided Mennonites from each other really stronger than those which united? What of the fact that all were strangers and pilgrims in an alien land, that Russia tolerated them for their economic productivity and not out of respect for their nonconformity? Should not external pressures generate a cohesiveness capable of overcoming internal religious differences? What of the common life experience in the context of the village? Mennonites still ate the same food, slept in similar houses and farmed in a uniform way. Ultimately different religious persuasions co-existed in one socio-economic frame. In this setting there were fortunately a number of forces which conspired to break down barriers.

One of these coincided with the emergence of the Brethren. By the mid-nineteenth century rapid population growth had shattered the social and economic tranquility of the old settlements. The rapid absorption of reserve land created a group of landless Mennonites which at times comprised over half the population. In the late 1860s a systematic resettlement gradually provided a solution to the population surplus and the severe social tensions it produced. This colonization within Russia generally improved inter-Mennonite relations. Economic cooperation was essential to survival on the new frontier, be it the Kuban, Sagradovka or Siberia. Droughts which withered crops; diseases that decimated livestock; nomadic people who resented the settlement of their grazing lands—such collective difficulties possibly made particular views on the nature of salvation or the mode of baptism seem less important. In the Kuban the Brethren shared their house of worship with Mennonite Templars who rejected baptism and the Lord's Supper as "false sacred relics."[8] At times the frontier was almost too religiously liberating. One colonist, reporting on the status of four Mennonite villages in Siberia, observed that "Old Church Brethren, Alliance,

Adventists and free thinkers (Templars?) are all represented here, yet all are good Mennonites."[9] It was nevertheless disconcerting when the Adventists shattered the Sunday calm by starting a threshing machine, "but what can be done if we want freedom of conscience."[10]

Unfortunately such frontier diversity was often completely without religious leadership. Initially there was no minister in the ten villages of the Memrik settlement. Much the same problem prevailed in the eleven villages of the Pavlodar settlement in 1908.[11] In both these instances Brethren ministers at first served all groups. In some settlements these circumstances laid the basis for long term cooperation. Joint worship services, Bible conferences, choirs and ministerial courses were commonplace in the Siberian settlements.[12] In the Sagradovka colony ministers from both the Brethren and the Old Church often served village congregations alternately. Thanksgiving festivals were carefully scheduled so that the members of both groups could attend all the services. Participation in common mission projects was the order of the day.[13] In Sagradovka this sense of cooperation and greater belonging even transcended a rather steady loss of Old Church members, including ministers, to the Brethren and in later years, to the Evangelical Mennonite Church.

After 1880 the practice of nonresistance—Russian Mennonite style—played a rather diverse role in inter-Mennonite relations. The ideal of nonviolence basically found expression in the operation of the forestry service with its defined obligations and procedure. Its support demanded a high level of cooperation from all Mennonite groups. Though a key issue of faith its expression was specifically defined and so nonresistance generated no common theological meeting ground capable of bringing the Old Church and the Brethren closer together. There was another devisive element, especially for the Brethren. Forestry service was demanded of all young Mennonite males, regardless of personal conviction. The resulting mix of believer and unbeliever combined with the relative youth of most recruits made it difficult to exercise effective social control in the camps. Some even considered the forestry service as "a primary station for our home missions."[14] Ministerial consultations as well as All-Mennonite conferences frequently agonized about the lack of religious piety in the camps. It was difficult to create a common basis of faith in this setting, even with the help of forestry chaplains and itinerant ministers.

As an expression of nonviolence the forestry service had its limitations: its sense of compulsion; its isolation from the rest of society; its lack of active involvement with human suffering. There was nevertheless a compensating factor. Among its participants it created a sense of comradery which transcended denominational lines. When a Russian Mennonite spoke of his *Forstei Brueder* (Forestry Brothers) it never mattered which church they belonged to. The many *Forstei* reunions of later decades speak eloquently to the unifying effect of a common life in the barracks. Here was a sense of peoplehood unattainable in the context of conventional religion.

A common debt also united Mennonite groups in the early twentieth century. When Mennonite state service commenced in 1880 its cost was entirely borne by the Mennonites. At first the system was financed through a head tax as well as an assessment based on land holdings. In time the revenue base was broadened to include businessmen and industrialists. Finally, by 1909 a universal tax levied on all Mennonite property, private and corporate, came into effect. The new forestry tax was based on the individual's net worth. When the deficits continued, the tax was placed on the same footing as any other state levies and collectable by force if necessary. In this setting Mennonite leaders of all persuasions frequently met to deal with the problems confronting the Forestry Commission. It was not, however, a platform for resolving doctrinal differences.

Likewise cooperation during WWI was not necessarily the result of a better theological understanding between Mennonite groups. Even the Mennonites were caught up in the wave of patriotism sweeping over Russia at the onset of the conflict. Everywhere villages and volosts collected food, clothing and monies for the needy families of Russian conscripts or use in field hospitals and general relief. Initially some young Mennonites volunteered for the Red Cross. Conscription soon placed others in the forestry or noncombatant medical service. This diaspora of unprecedented magnitude not only meant that Mennonites of every kind and description were thrown together, but that they were also scattered throughout the length and breadth of Russia. What happened to the impressionable young when they witnessed the carnage on Russia's western front or the plight of the peasant in rural Russia? Perhaps the religious differences which seemed so crucial at the village level lapsed into insignificance. A suffering world only asked for solace, not a specific brand of Mennonitism. The intense period of cooperation which followed war and revolution, though prompted by a concern with collective survival, was spiritually enhanced by the presence of men and women who experienced something of the larger world. Here was a further stretching of the Russian Mennonite mind-set which supplemented the cultural broadening of earlier decades.

As the nineteenth century drew to a close all Mennonites faced the crucial question of cultural survival. For several decades their sense of German identity had been reinforced by a significant minority of future teachers travelling to Germany and Switzerland for pedagogical training. Others obtained their professional qualifications in Russian institutions. At times it seemed there was a potential for a bilingual culture. In the end the pace of acculturation became unmanageable. With the accession of Alexander III nationalistic pressures demanded that Russian become the language of instruction in Mennonite schools. Increasingly local school boards lost their autonomy in setting the curriculum and appointing teachers. Only the concessions granted by the October Manifesto in 1905 momentarily halted the erosion of this key link in the Russian Mennonite sense of identity.

Such threats of assimilation naturally forced greater inter-Mennonite cooperation. Certainly the almost frantic founding of new schools and the intense upgrading of teacher qualifications early in the twentieth century could be interpreted as an effort to block absorption into slavic culture. The majority of the religious and cultural ideas which provided a sense of Russian-Mennonite peoplehood were sustained in the context of the German language. In such a setting religious differences might well become secondary to the common task of preserving traditional life patterns and piety. The school, the historic transmitter of Mennonite ideals and practices, was the obvious means of cultural and intellectual assertion and both Brethren and Old Church members were very much a part of its operation.

There was another less obvious dimension associated with the school which directly affected inter-Mennonite relations. While the Brethren were restricting their borders on such issues as open communion and the acceptance of immersed believers only, a different scenario was unfolding in the minds of many of their teachers. The ideas of Rousseau were finally reaching the Mennonite teacher on the Russian steppes. Johann Heinrich Pestalozzi had been profoundly influenced by Rousseau's *Emile* on the one hand and by his old teacher Bodmer, a rabid Swiss

84

patriot, on the other.[15] Thanks to these influences Pestalozzi not only praised the inherent virtue of the peasant but argued that his education was the only means of revitalizing a stagnant and stratified society. All men had natural gifts and powers, provided the educator awakened them. It was not surprising that this interest in the life of the village struck a sympathetic cord on the Russian plains.

The educational fervor which emerged during the first decade of the 20th century created a new constituency among the Russian Mennonites which cut across denominational lines. While not unrelated to the religious ecumenicalism which characterized the *Allianz* movement, the new mood also exhibited secular overtones. Instruction in reading, writing, arithmetic and Bible history was sanctioned by long standing practice. But what about adding the history of literature, poetry, and drawing to the curriculum?[16] The study of German and Russian was naturally imperative, but what of English and French? *Heimatkunde* naturally included the study of geography as well as local plant and animal life, but was it essential to know Russian and German fairy tales? Why did the Molotschna Mennonite School Society affirm that "more light folk songs were needed" in the music curriculum at its 12th annual meeting in 1911?[17] There was more. Young women should be sent to Germany in order to study Froebel Kindergartens and female teachers were to be allowed in the regular schools.[18] Was it the subversive effect of the books which began to accumulate on the shelves of the teacher societies? Some of these naturally focused on weighty themes like pedagogy, history and literature. Others seemed more frivolous— adventure, travel and fiction.[19] According to some educators there was even a need for something more—"fresh air, plenty of light and reasonable physical exercise."[20]

Were the Mennonite peasants of the Russian steppes to be transformed into an educated elite? Where was the orthodox piety of old, the precisely defined ethic, the exacting division between the secular and the sacred? The mind-set of these new "humanists" frequently transcended the borders of their respective group, but because their reforms were gradual and transpired in the context of community they did not threaten the prevailing equilibrium. Tremendous advances had occurred in business and agriculture and it seemed fitting to extend this to learning as well.

Judging from the minutes of the various teacher societies there is one thing they did not do—engage in serious religious

85

dialogue. For that matter neither did the annual All-Mennonite conferences. Their agendas covered benevolent institutions, schools, missions and the forestry service, but there were no study conferences dealing with mutual views on the nature of salvation or the concept of the church. Similarly the sermons published in *Friedensstimme* and *Der Botschafter* were piously devotional, but carefully avoided any discussion of key theological matters. If confrontation occurred at all, the issues were external and minor: closed communion; the Brethren flirtation with the Baptists; marriage across confessional lines; the reluctance of the Brethren to invite ministers from the Old Church.

Dialogue finally did take place, but it began in Germany, not Russia. At first it was the Brethren who were primarily involved. The issue was their association with the Blankenburg *Allianz* conferences in Germany. Mennonite Brethren already attended these conferences in the 1890s and by 1900 some aspects of this theological orientation emerged at the Brethren annual conferences. A dissenting minority raised questions concerning the Brethren insistence that only immersed believers were elegible to share in communion. Some of the liberal elements joined the *Allianz* or at least cooperated with it.

Generally speaking, the influence of the *Allianz* affected Brethren—Old Church relations positively. It was the *Allianz* concept of *Gemeinschaft* (fellowship) in its uniquely German connotation which helped to break down the barriers between the Russian Mennonites. The *Allianz*, by stressing the inner spirit and minimizing external form allowed like-minded Mennonites to cooperate on many fronts. An awareness of those socially outcast came not only came from F.W. Badeker's preaching tours and his ministry in Russia's northern exile camps and prisons but from the German models of old age homes, orphanages, deaf-mute schools and mental hospitals. In the new setting interested Mennonites joined together in the work of the Molotschna Tract Society, various relief committees, the support of evangelists in both Russian and Mennonite villages, tent missions and the distribution of broadranging devotional literature. After the Brethren joined the All-Mennonite Conference in 1906 they participated in discussions relating to support for foreign missions, *Reiseprediger* (itinerant preachers), forestry commando chaplaincies, and even discussion concerning a joint seminary to ensure better trained ministers.

In 1910 H.J. Braun of the Brethren observed that both groups had identical views on Scripture, divorce, the oath, congregational democracy, nonresistance and adult baptism.[21] It was time to admit that a "true vital Christianity"[22] now existed in the Old Church. When asked to explain Mennonite divisions to a representative of the Ministry of the Interior, the Gnadenfeld elder and veteran missionary Heinrich Dirks explained that the *Kirchliche* (Old Church) were Old Mennonites, the Brethren, Mennonites and the Evangelical Mennonite Brethren, New Mennonites. They agreed on the basic Christian issues: the new life in Christ and baptism of faith. Minor questions need not hinder unification.[23]

Dirk's plea for unity in essentials reflects a rather vigorous discussion of several issues among members of the Old Church. What of the formalism associated with baptism, at times practiced without faith and as a prerequisite to marriage in the church? Was baptism always a mass affair and did it always have to fall on one day?[24] It was important to stress the inner meaning of baptism, not the external form.[25] Faith, not tradition, was the true prerequisite for baptism. Old Church adherents also focused on the nature of the believers' church. Some tried to distinguish between a religious peoplehood in which most were eventually admitted to baptism and communion, and the committed believers within that group. It was not easy. One discussant complained: "We are neither *Volkskirche* nor a church of believers."[26] The Gnadenfeld minister Jakob Janzen was more emphatic: "We are *Volkskirche* and want to be that."[27] The best one could do, he argued, was to stay and work from within. In keeping with the existing structure it was perhaps even useful to dedicate children as Mennonites, then later baptize them on faith as Christians.[28]

Allianz with its theology of essentials, a united social action on many fronts, a long-standing forestry service, a broad based commitment to home and foreign missions—the split persisted. Why? One is tempted to blame the Brethren, especially when sampling the documents of the early twentieth century. They insisted that only immersed believers share in their communion service; that every baptismal candidate be carefully scrutinized; that, as a rule, Old Church ministers not speak in their services; finally, there was a strong church discipline at times characterized by self-righteousness and legalism. Religious exactness and the occasional sense of moral superiority made the Brethren unapproachable.

Such an interpretation is probably too simplistic. Thanks to a broad- ranging Mennonite institutionalism and the revivalistic theology of the *Allianz*, the pre-WWI Russian Mennonites stood closer to one another than at any time since the split of 1860. They were certainly more tolerant of each other than their co-religionists in North America. What basic issue kept them apart?

An Old Church adherent writing in 1912 possibly provides an answer.[29] Johann Janzen was extremely critical of his own group. It had, he argued, lost the concept of the believer's church and its essential component, the "pure church."

> Since we, as already has been said, have defected from the ideal of a pure church (*einer... reinen Gemeinde*), it is little wonder that we are not exacting about instituting the same.... Why do the healthy remain with the sick? We want to take them all with us—all without exceptions. This idea that all Mennonites and their children have to be brought into the church of Christ—this idea weakens us. It has transformed our churches into hybrid churches; to a degree it has alienated us from the original Mennonitism; it gives us the idea God wants *Volkskirchen*; it has made us forget that the Bible speaks of calling, election, chosen ones and saints.[30]

The crisis confronting inter-Mennonite relations involved more than individuals and groups. It revolved around the classic problem confronting Christian sectarianism in any age. What happens after one obeys the injunction to "come out from among them"? The Russian Mennonites were victims of a long historical process. In pursuit of the pure church they had through the decades separated themselves from the state churches. Once apart they found that the *Volkskirche* tradition, to which they took exception, re-established itself in their midst. Once again the church accepted all who were born into its political and social order. In the 1860s both the Brethren and the Old Church clearly understood the dilemma. One argued that the new life could not be lived in the old setting, while the other feared that the exodus of the serious pilgrim might disrupt the existing community. Both views exacted consequences. The Brethren were tempted to make a pure church purer, and so generally defined the nature of the Christian walk rather precisely. The Old Church, which remained co-extensive with society, agonized about the difficulty of nurturing the serious believer when many others in the same group remained less committed. They in effect said: "This is what we are, so let us make the best of it," to which the Brethren responded: "This is what we can be, let us strive to attain it."

Who were the truly righteous in the Russian Mennonite world of say, 1910? Surely the call for a theology of essentials, the increasing economic affluence and the widespread contact with the outside world demanded changes in the definition of what constituted the pure church. Religious awakenings and the influence of *Allianz* piety gradually changed the character of the Old Church. There was a sincere agonizing about narrowing the prevailing definition of the believers' church, but the prevailing structures apparently dictated the continuation of the status quo. The conservatives among the Brethren instinctively restricted the circle of the elect. Immersion continued to be viewed as the only correct baptismal mode, the formula for *Bekehrung* remained tightly prescribed, and communion services admitted immersed believers only. In protest some liberal Brethren joined the *Allianz* and the movement became something of a half-way house between the two opposing views on the nature of the believers' church.

In the end it was impossible to agree on a common definition of the "truly righteous" in the Russian setting. Historically each group had developed its own sense of religious peoplehood. One stressed that it lay primarily in the *Gemeinschaft* (fellowship) practiced in the local *Gemeinde* (congregation). The other, while using the same terms, applied them to a more diffuse community. Each group was secure in its concept of the believers' church. It was futile to argue who was right and who was wrong. Each instinctively understood its own perimeters. Each knew on what levels cooperation was possible and where it was not. By l914 such a modus vivendi set the stage for widespread cooperation and goodwill, but not reunification.

NOTES

Some of the material in this Chapter was previously published as "Brethren and Old Church Relations in Pre-World War I Russia: Setting the Stage for Canada," *Journal of Mennonite Studies*, II (1984), 42-59. I want to thank the journal for permission to use this material.

[1] P.M. Friesen, *Die Alt-Evangelische Mennonitische Bruederschaft in Russland 1789-1910* (Halbstadt, Taurien, 1911), 268-269.
[2] Jacob Epp Diary (Mennonite Heritage Centre, Winnipeg, Manitoba), May 12, 1862. See also Friesen, 269-272.
[3] Jacob Epp Diary, June 11, 1962; also Friesen, 275-278.
[4] Friesen, 269, 276.

5 D. Epp, "Wie kann das moeglich sein?" *Der Botschafter VIII* (1910), no. 53, 2-3; no. 54, 3.
6 A few of the reports of itinerant ministers were published by P.M. Friesen. Many more can be found in the *Zionsbote*, which published them on a regular basis. See for example Hermann Neufeld, "Russland, Nikolaijewka, im Maerz, 1895," *Zionsbote*, XI (1895), no. 17, 2; Heinrich Friesen, "Reisebericht," *Zionsbote*, XI (1895), no. 18, 2.
7 D. Epp, "Wie kann das moeglich sein?" *Der Botschafter VII* (1910), no. 53, 2-3; no. 54, 3.
8 Isaak Fast, *Friedensstimme*, V(1907), no. 40, 514-515.
9 "Gljaden, Siberia," *Friedensstimme*, XI (1913), no. 10, 6.
10 *Ibid.*
11 W. Neufeld, "Eine Sibirienreise," *Friedensstimme*, VI(1908), no. 34, 537.
12 G. Fast, *In den Steppen Sibiriens* (Rosthern, Sask., n.d.), 74-79.
13 Gerhard Lohrenz, *Sagradowka* (Rosthern, Sask., 1947), 64-81.
14 Isack Ediger, "Was machen wir mit unsern Forsteien?" *Friedensstimme*, VII (1909), no. 30, 4-6.
15 See Josef Reinhart, *Heinrich Pestalozzi* (Basel, n.d.).
16 See for example "Protokoll der Konferenz der Zentralschullehrer in New York am 2. und 3. August 1910," *Friedensstimme*, VIII (1910), no. 64, 3-5.
17 "Protokoll der 12. allg. Versammlung des M.M. Lehrervereines am 14. Mai 1911 in Rueckenau," *Friedensstimme*, IX (1911), no. 43, 3-4. See also Protokoll der Lehrerkonferenz in Schoenfeld am 11. September 1910," *Friedensstimme*, VIII (1910), no. 8, 7.
18 "Protokoll der allgemeinen Mitgliederversammlung des Mennonitischen Mittelschulvereins am 6 August, 1910," *Friedensstimme*, VIII (1910),no. 63, 6.
19 "Protokoll der 10. allgem. Versammlung... des M.M. Lehrervereins am 19. und 20. August 1910 in Rueckenau," *Friedensstimme*, VIII (1910), no. 68, 2-3.
20 "Protokoll ueber die Schlusskonferenz der Lehrer des Schoenfelder Gebietes am 6 Mai, 1910 in Schoenfeld," *Friedensstimme*, VIII (1910), no. 24, 4-5.
21 H.J. Braun, "Mennoniten oder Baptisten?" *Friedensstimme*, VIII (1910), no. 3, 3-5.
22 *Ibid.*, 5.
23 "Offener Brief des Aeltesten H. Dirks," *Der Botschafter*, V(1910), no. 91, 3-4.
24 "Tauffreiheit und Taufzwang," *Der Botschafter*, VI (1911), no. 64, 3-4.
25 D. Epp, "Tauffreiheit und Taufzwang," *Der Botschafter*, VI (1911), no. 66, 3-4.
26 "Tauffreiheit und Taufzwang," *Der Botschafter*, VI(1911), no. 72, 3.
27 Jakob Janzen, "Noch Einiges uber Tauffreiheit und Taufzwang," *Der Botschafter*, VI(1911), no. 96, 4.
28 *Ibid.*
29 Johann Janzen, "Separatisten," *Der Botschafter* VII(1912), no. 22, 2-3; no. 23; 2-3.
30 *Ibid.*, no. 23, 2.

EPILOGUE

The few surviving records of Brethren beginnings tell very little about the inner spiritual journey which transformed ordinary villagers into radical dissenters. The documents related to the secession registered concerns about the indiscriminate mixing of believer and unbeliever in the overall life of the church. There were calls for a community of believers committed to personal faith and serious discipleship. Official proclamations likely concealed much of the drama associated with religious rediscovery. One thing is certain. The few intimate documents published in P.M. Friesen's massive study suggest that the early Brethren were deeply sincere in their search for new life and readily endured any censure or suffering associated with their quest. Some of their expectations and demands, however, could not be accommodated by the larger constituency under any circumstances.

All Mennonites in the Russian setting, whether nominally or passionately religious, found themselves in a political structure which they were powerless to change. The laws governing settlement confined them to self-contained communities while their classification as a religious group made them all Christian. The Old Church could not extricate itself from the community as a whole and choose to serve it to the best of its ability. It nourished traditional life patterns with its worship services, festival celebrations, periodic communion and annual baptism. In this setting a separatistic church meant an end to community solidarity.

The Brethren emerged in a Mennonite world characterized by varying shades of grey rather than the black and white categories depicted in some of their early pronouncements. While the majority of Mennonites endorsed the religious status quo there were still serious seekers in the old Church like Bernhard Harder, who tried to reform the system from within. Their protests were voiced before the secession and continued afterward. Some of these supported the Brethren call to repentance and conversion, but felt their demand for a separated church threatened family and community. Unfortunately the ensuing dialogue was not between the spiritually like-minded but involved antagonistic minorities. On one side stood the village or district mayors and some church elders, the one intent on upholding political stability, the other firmly committed to the sanctity of traditional religion. On the other side stood the spokesmen for the Brethren, pulsating with the joy of new found peace and determined to implement a new vision of the believers' church regardless of consequences. One called for public order, one for revival. They had difficulty hearing one another. Meaningful communication became impossible when a radical fringe insisted the Brethren divest themselves of their remaining religious traditions and engage in excessive celebrations of joy.

The spiritual violence associated with early Brethren dissent, especially the exuberance movement, did little permanent damage. The rapid normalization following the June Reforms was an eloquent testimony to the moderate theology of most secessionists. The long term balance between experience and discipleship generated considerable vitality in the Brethren pilgrimage during subsequent decades. Generally their concept of discipleship was shaped within the community, not imported from elsewhere. Evangelism and nurture occurred simultaneously within the congregation. Individualism had little opportunity to create aberrations or generate excesses. Itinerant ministers, annually elected by the constituency, owed their appointment to the fact that they reflected community norms and values. Their messages focused on the conversion and the ongoing pilgrimage, at least judging from the surviving sermons. All this was conducive to uniformity and stability. Little wonder that late nineteenth century converts extolled the intimate fellowship offered in Brethren congregations. By 1900 the Brethren possessed a firm sense of their own peoplehood and were heirs to an accumulative religious tradition.

Did the predictable home Bible studies, special festivals, ministerial visits and sermons possibly spawn a peoplehood which was too insular? There was the temptation to hold the line, to affirm old values and practices. Some of the Brethren may have been threatened by the rapid economic, intellectual and spiritual expansion of the Russian Mennonite world in the early twentieth century. The succession of ministers and Bible teachers from Germany presented a special dilemma. They preached an orthodox Gospel yet insisted on loose borders for the believers' church. As long as faith was present, they insisted, the baptismal mode should not bar the individual from communion participation. While a few Brethren embraced the new visions fomented by the *Allianz*, the many insisted on closed communion and threatened to excommunicate the liberals in their midst. It seemed that by 1910 a half century of growth and development once again produced orthodoxy. The style of house and worship services became sacrosanct. The path of conversion was precisely prescribed while the mode of baptism remained fixed. Such rigidity, while crippling, was not fatal to the vitality of congregational life. In the decades which followed, several developments, potentially restorative, gave the Brethren soul no rest.

There was the broad-ranging interest in education which not only saw the erection of schools at home but frequent individual study abroad or in Russian universities. Such intellectual expansion was theologically revitalizing insofar as it generated an awareness of world missions. Some of the Brethren now insisted on evangelism among the Russians. Since the conference was not officially committed to such a work, individual members, at the risk of hardship or imprisonment, dedicated themselves to this task. Their enthusiasm and example forced some Brethren out of their confinement.

The broadening cultural contacts, especially with Germany, generally sharpened the Russian-Mennonite social conscience. Most of the welfare institutions erected by 1914 were based on western European models. Brethren participation in such applied Christianity of necessity pried them away from the insular and experiential and forced them into a larger world arena.

There was another sequel. Open minded leaders from both the Old Church and the Brethren moved to institutionalize their cooperation. Interaction at Faith Conferences (*Glaubenskonferenzen*) and Bible Conferences (*Bibelbesprechungen*) was not only formalized in the organization of the *Allianz* but also in the Brethren affiliation with the All-Mennonite Conference at Schoensee, Molotschna, in 1910. Increasingly the Brethren now saw the Old Church not as corrupt and inadequate, but as a fellow pilgrim.

Finally, the upheaval generated by revolution, civil war and migration demanded a piety rooted in the reality of the everyday world. Whether individuals stayed or left, the traditional Mennonite and Brethren world was forever shattered. For both the comfort of the mother tongue, the safety of venerated customs and the security of established economic patterns disappeared forever. Now came the challenge of a discipleship capable of transcending dispersion. For some this meant loneliness and death in the labor camp, for others the isolation of the Canadian prairies or the Parguayan Chaco. Time proved a relentless taskmaster. The Brethren moved from the village to the city both in eastern Russia and in western North America. Once again they would have to find the balance between experience and discipleship, feeling and following.